Allowing Inspired Transformation

6 Steps to Defining Your Purpose for an Epic Effect

Dr. Jolene Church

Successful Thinking Mindset

ISBN: 978-0-578-99141-2

DEDICATION

To the man who captivated my heart decades ago and shares my thoughts and dreams, my husband Hawsie. I thank you for cheering me on and helping me complete this project. I love you.

To my family, I am blessed to have all of you as inspiration for all that I do. Thank you. I love you.

CONTENTS

ACKNOWLEDGEMENT

So many events happen in our lives that we don't bat an eye at until later. In hindsight we look in awe and say, "Oh my gosh, if I just would have paid attention." The point is, it doesn't matter if you listen now or listen later, the lesson that you are intended to receive will happen, sometimes over and over – until you get it.

Thank you, Grandma Gloria – I get it. I love you.

INTRODUCTION

Throughout time, people have questioned the reason for their existence. Philosophies have been developed, examining the nature and purpose of being. You would think someone would have figured all this out by now. Yet still the search to answer the existential question has not waned - Why I am here?

The answer to this question is much closer than it seems. Our existence is a unique experience, and one that is custom designed for each and every one of us. We are in no way "cookie-cutter" or the same because the events and circumstance, regardless of how similar, are unique experiences to every person.

Over the course of several decades, I have helped people tap into their uniqueness, their "it". I have personally coached hundreds of individuals and helped thousands through group trainings and workshops identify their purpose and develop actionable plans to begin living in their purpose and experience fulfillment in their lives.

In 2002, the Purpose Driven Life phenomenon, based on the book of the same name, by Pastor Rick Warren took the U.S. and world by storm. People longing to figure out 'why' and knowing that there was more to life, devoted themselves to living a purpose driven life.

Today, decades later, people are still search for their purpose, to figure out what it is and how to live in it. We are told that you must "find" your purpose. But where do you even begin to look?

Each and every one of us has unique experiences that serve as our school in developing our skills, talents, and strengths. As we experience happiness and pain, our skillset grows, preparing us for our path, our meaning, and our purpose.

This book is a guide to help you finally figure it all out and sort through what doesn't seem to make sense as well as what you know is important. Your purpose is not something that you need to search for and find. Rather, it simply needs to be defined. From there, you just need a solid action plan to get you from here to there. I can help with that. That is what I do and what I was put on this planet to help you with.

If you are ready to begin this journey, I'm ready to help you get to the place that you desire – living in your purpose, on purpose, so that you can live your best life. Let's dig in.

CHAPTER 1

DEFINING FULFILLMENT

"There is a powerful driving force inside every human being that once unleashed can make any vision, dream or desire a reality." ~ Anthony Robbins

I love the above quote as it reminds me that I am responsible for turning my desires into reality and my reality into success. I have the power to dream big and to do great things. Success is an amazing thing. But what is success? How do we achieve success? And why do some people seem more successful than others?

Let's start by sorting out what success is so that we can get to a point where you can identify not only what success looks like and feels like to you, but more importantly what is your secret success sauce. We often buy into other's beliefs of success and in the process lose sight of our authenticity and purpose.

Renowned mindfulness instructor Mare Chapman refers to this process of comparison as "othering". This is the automatic mental movement of attention away from the self to the other based on the assumption that the other has more power, authority or, to our point, success. Some people may seem to have a magical success formula in which everything they touch turns to gold. This in contrast to other folks who seemingly have one bad break after another. Do we randomly win some and lose some or do we have an inherent secret sauce?

Imagine how our creativity, ingenuity and special qualities combine to invoke something deep inside us to form our secret sauce and start us on a path to success. Look around the room you are sitting in right now and notice how other individual's secret sauce is coating everything around us. Likely you notice a phone, furniture, a clock or perhaps a television set. You are literally surrounded by someone's success. Every shred of paper was based on an idea that eventually led to success. We are surrounded by success and thus success is inescapable.

So why is it that so many people are confused about the definition of success? Is it a certain level of income? Is it a fancy car? Is it anything materialistic at all? The reason why so many people cannot define success is because success is an outcome. It is the result of a feeling, and sometimes feelings are not based on reality. They derive from a thought (real or unreal) which creates a feeling. Our lives are mostly affected by the way we think things are, not the way they are. Success is the result of a thought or a story that we are telling ourselves, such as, "I've finally made it" A statement like that is surely going to develop a feeling. You "feel" successful because you told yourself so; but is it true?

I cannot tell you what success feels like for you because I can only do me. My thoughts and beliefs on success are based in my values and desires. Your truth, at least what you might tell yourself is your truth, develops your feelings. This is the reason when you ask a group of people what success is to them, it's all over the place. To some it is things, to others happiness and to others it is a destination. Unfortunately, I am here to drop a bomb on you and tell you that they are all right, at least in their minds because it is their truth. This said, success relies on your secret sauce, your *it*.

For decades, I have been quite curious as to what *it* is and its relationship with success. I can tell you that it didn't matter whether I was analyzing people in large corporations or my next-door neighbor, *it* became quite evident. There was no escaping *it*. *It*, when defined, was the secret ingredient to success. The more I studied people, the more I understood *it* and how to help people find *it* within themselves. This included studying myself.

In 1988, Nike launched the *Just Do It*™ campaign. Nike left the interpretation of *it* up to the consumer. Some 30 plus years later, people can still be heard proclaiming, "Just do it!" This tag line became a mantra for some and a way of life for others. It remains an all-time recognizable catch phrase. For some "Just do it" became a personal challenge to take on fears and obstacles in pursuit of success. People connected to its simplicity, yet its richness became such a driving force for people around the world.

The success of the Nike campaign was rooted in a motivational proclamation to not allow your head to get in your way. Don't listen to what others are telling you. If you want it, you can have it. Dig deep, commit, and take a leap of faith. Just do it! And this mantra wasn't reserved for athletes. Just do it served as an awakening for young and old alike. If you want success you have to go for it, go after it. And in the doing, just doing, you are exercising your *it*.

Still, I have not exactly told you what *it* is. Let me first tell you what it is not.

It is not luck, chance or happenstance. Nor is *it* based on social status, economics, or what side of the tracks you were born. *It* cannot be taken from you, but you can have a hard time finding *it* and *it* can feel lost. Put in the most basic terms, *it* resides in the raw, unadulterated, real, authentic you and the way we get to *it*, define *it*, and understand *it* is through inspired translation, which then becomes inspired transformation; transforming your thoughts so that you are inspired by your special gifts.

Our *it* is what makes us special, what makes us unique. We may be cut from a similar cloth, but the patterns and the stitching are different. There is no other you. There is no other person that shares what you have inside. Your *it* is uniquely designed for you. And your *it* is what makes you stand out.

For me, I can think back on some of my earliest childhood memories and can clearly see my *it*. But hindsight is 20/20, right? For me, and I assure you, for you, your *it* is likely just as evident.

When I was three years old, I had my first *brilliant* business idea. I lived in the Los Angeles, California suburb of Glendale in a wonderful little craftsman style house blocks from the freeway overpass that lead to the tall buildings of downtown Glendale. I don't have many memories of my time in that house, but one memory stands out, and that was the day I decided to make my own money. Yes, a three-year old entrepreneur.

I can clearly remember walking down the front walk

toward the street. It was a beautiful day, neither hot nor cold. It was the perfect day to start a business. Hanging a right up the sidewalk, I confidently walked several blocks up to a busy intersection that led to the freeway overpass. Many people were driving and walking past. Perfect! I had a plan and I set out to make money. A business idea was born and launched on the same day.

Earlier that week, my mom had accidently gifted me business equipment. And in my mind, it was a magic money machine! You see, when I was little, gas stations were service stations. You didn't go to the service station and just get gas. Instead, service attendants checked the oil level in your car, tire pressure, and washed the windshield. I know full-service gas stations still exist in some places today, but I haven't seen these in California for decades. When I was a kid, these were the norm. I loved watching the attendants. The best part was when they were done. My mom would hand the attendant a plastic card and they would place the card on a little blue clipboard about the size of a large index card. The attendant would place a multi-layered piece of paper over the card and the attendant would slide a plastic handle over the clipboard past the paper. The machine would make a funny KACHINK sound. The attendant would hand my mom the money machine and a pen. She would sign the paper and hand the machine back to him.

"What is that?" I asked.

"That's how I pay the man," she responded.

I was fascinated! How was this so? I didn't see money. My mom never gave the man any money, as I knew it. Clearly at three I knew what money was. I was a member of Glendale Federal Saving's Squirrel Club! I had coin savings cards full of money. I loved collecting money, so I was always looking for ways to get more.

One day my mom had somehow forgotten to hand back the magic blue money machine before leaving the station. When she realized what she had done, she was already home. She called the station and let them know that she would bring it back next time she was out. But for now, BINGO! I had just been set up for business!

As I watched the passers-by, I will never forget my first customer. He was a tall, slender gentleman with brown hair and a kind smile. As he approached, he had no idea how he was about to be wowed by the impeccable sales pitch of this 3-foot tall, brown-eyed pip squeak. As he got within a foot, I beamed a bright smile from ear to ear. And then – show time! I had seen this a million times.

I outstretched my magic blue money machine, loaded with paper in one hand and a pen in the other to him as I began my sales pitch.

"If you give me a dime, you can sign my paper."

Perplexed, the stranger couldn't help but smile. "Excuse me?"

Clearly, he wasn't the brightest bulb in the box, but I had seen this work again and again. Let me try again.

"If you give me a dime, you can sign my paper."

To that, the man reached in his pocket, searched around and pulled out a handful of change. He quickly sorted through the coins in open palm and selected out several of the little silver discs that I had come to enjoy collecting. I outstretched my hand and he placed what felt like a million dimes in my little hand. Wow! If the guys at the service station could see me now. I quickly slid the plastic handle across the magic money machine. KACHINK! The satisfaction of my first customer and first sale!

Unsuspecting passer-by after passer-by were wooed by my amazing sales pitch. To my complete surprise, not one person actually signed the paper but ALL of them gave me money! And with each sale, KACHINK! Magic! If the guys at the service station could see how I improved their process. They were doing it all wrong.

There is no clue how long I was out on that busy street corner that day, but it seemed like all day. The customers just kept coming, so I just kept smiling and selling. It was awesome.

The pile of coins came as quite a shock to my parents. I proudly told them about my business venture. I described my sales pitch and how I improved how the magic money machine worked. I recanted how all I had to do was smile and ask people for money and they responded positively.

I was a natural. Dimes rained down from heaven that day. Heck, a dime in those days could buy a kid two candy bars. I was rich! Somehow, without even having a kindergarten education, I had figured out that making money was easy. I was confident and proud of my accomplishment. An entrepreneur was born.

Looking at the situation from the perspective of a parent myself, I would have been horrified if my child came home and proudly exclaimed that she'd been panhandling on the street corner. But in my mind, as a bright-eyed three-year old, I had no fear to approach strangers and do what I had seen the attendants do on a regular basis. I had simply started a business.

Unfortunately, the doors to my business closed as quickly as it had opened. After telling my parents where I had been and what I had done, I wasn't allowed to run my business anymore and I was shut down. To think, my first business adventure, a true success! The feeling of accomplishment, that was success. I had accomplished what I set out to do; what I believed I could do. It wasn't money that was success, it was the feeling derived.

This little story helps provide some insight into how I

discovered my *it*. I'm a natural goal-setter, entrepreneur, and process improver. I'm not afraid of taking chances and going for it. The feeling that I derived that day was a sense of satisfaction because I employed my natural talents. One of my greatest qualities remains today, having faith in what I believe in. This is a driving force for me.

Over the course of several decades, helping people find their *it* has become a passion of mine. Helping people tap into their inner strengths, passions and uniqueness so that they can live their dreams and live their best life is what I was put on this planet to do, and I'm thrilled to take you on this journey.

Here is a small exercise that I like to use on my clients to begging tapping into their passions and motivations. This is an exercise to start pulling into the layers of what makes you, distinctly you. Don't fret if it seems confusing at first. We will dig in, layer by layer until we discover your *it* and allow in *inspired transformation*.

Imagine that you have a fairy godmother, and she can grant you exactly what you ask for. She asks you, "If you could do anything in the world and be paid extravagantly for what you do, regardless of whether or not the job you select warrants extravagant pay, what would you choose?"

Most people struggle with this question. It's usually easier when you think of an industry or something specific. Think about what you enjoy and ask yourself a *wouldn't it be great question.* You know, those are the times when you say, "Wouldn't it be great if we could.....?" What is your "*wouldn't it be great*?" What would you love to do to produce an income if supporting yourself was not an issue?

You might have a desire to do something artistic. "Wouldn't it be great if I could make pottery for a living? I'd have a studio filled with big windows and the sun would beam in as I sit with my hands in clay on the potter's wheel."

You might have a desire to do something that requires many hours of training and experience, like a pilot. "Wouldn't it be great to be a pilot and fly private jets all over the world?"

You might have a desire to serve others in despair. "Wouldn't it be great to bring a smile to someone's face that is down and has lost all hope?"

You might want to build skyscrapers, race cars, or take care of animals. We all have untapped desires and dreams. Within our "wouldn't it be greats" lives our passion. You may have never been near a race car or even known a pilot, so what is it that you find so alluring? You desire something exciting? Relaxing? Satisfying? These are the outcomes of success. The feelings of success.

Until you understand your desires, motivators and driving factors, you are easily susceptible to succumbing to the influence of others on your thinking and the influence of your current situation or circumstance on your thinking. Your desires and driving factors may shift to adapt, taking you away from your true, authentic self. Your special qualities reside in the authentic you and help you in moving toward what you desire. Let me illustrate.

I naturally love people. At three-years old, I recognized the importance of connection through non-verbal cues. I greeted my customers with a genuine smile. I welcomed them in, connecting through a smile. My true authentic self, full of confidence and belief in my abilities, shined as I shared a big grin with my customers. This hasn't changed as I've grown into adulthood. My authentic, curious, confident self has helped me find what it is that I excel at and has helped me to find my purpose.

Finding you, the authentic you, can feel like a daunting

task, but will free you to finally live the life you've always dreamed of, a life of fulfillment. Let's get started.

CHAPTER 2

ILLUMINATING WHAT'S INSIDE

"If you are always trying to be normal, you will never know how amazing you can be." ~ Maya Angelou

When I was growing up, we moved more than any other family that I knew. About every three or four months we packed up our belongings and off we went to a new house. Sometimes the move was in town and other times to a completely different part of the state. Once, the move entailed a 1250-mile journey from San Diego, California to Seattle, Washington.

After packing up in just a matter of days, with my cat Mittens and her newborn kittens in tow, we ended up pretty much taking a *U-Haul vacation.* The home my parents intended to buy was sold the night before we got to Seattle. I've been told since I never actually lived there and only stayed in a motel for 10 days while we were trying to find a home that this doesn't count as a move.

Let's just say that it was a vacation disguised as a move.

Moving was hard. It meant packing up everything. Not just my stuff, but the dishes, towels and knick-knacks. The things that made a house feel like a home. I became a pro at finding boxes. I got way too good at packing. To this day, I hate moving regardless how good I am at organizing and packing.

Moving meant saying goodbye to the friends I had been able to make in my short time wherever *there* was. It also meant making a new friend quickly as a matter of survival. No kid wants to play alone at recess or not have someone to sit with at lunch. I dreaded each new school experience. But I loved school and acquiring knowledge and I was good at it.

By now you are probably wondering if I was a military brat. The answer is no. We just moved – a lot. I like to see the reaction on people's faces when I make the statement "My family was in a witness protection program."

The reality was that my parents easily become bored with where they were. Since we were renting there was nothing holding us down. I changed schools 33 times between kindergarten and twelfth grade. I graduated high-school early when I turned 18 because I could not bear another day of the torture that school had become to me. It was a drudgery day in and day out.

While other kids in my senior class were planning senior pictures, prom, and what college they were going to, I was just trying to figure out how to get out. I felt that I was being held back from what I needed to be doing, what I needed to be learning, and what I wanted to do. But what the heck did I want to do?

At nine years old I wanted to be a veterinarian and at fourteen a fashion merchandiser. At eighteen I had no clue. This may resonate with many of you. I remember watching my kids graduate high school and thinking just how ludicrous it seemed when looking into schools that they needed to know what they wanted to do with the rest of their lives. Later, as a university professor, I counselled adult graduate students who were still trying to figure it all out. Same thing as a human resource professional. Finally, as a business consultant and executive coach, the same old existential questions kept being posed: "What is my purpose? Is this as good as it gets? Do I have this all wrong? Am I destined to just work with no joy? Shouldn't my work be fulfilling?"

What the heck? What I have discovered probably won't come as a shock, but there are MANY fundamentals that are NOT taught in traditional school curriculum. One of those fundamentals is how to embrace your authentic you. You don't learn how to identify how to take your strengths and passions to help guide you to find your uniqueness (your *it*) and find a career that is fulfilling and doesn't feel like work, because it's not; it's an extension of you.

Rest assured I can help you learn what you didn't. It will take some work on your part but the benefits that you will reap as you find greater meaning from the world around you as you figure it out will be worth the work you put into the process.

Going back to the move. I didn't share that story for you to feel sorry for me, but instead to illustrate the impact that events and circumstances can have on your life. I never quite understood each move. It was a pain in the rear to move. I hated leaving my friends and the uneasiness I felt with each new school. If I was content and joyful why disrupt that again and again?

Perhaps the most important point about my extreme moving experience and being the new kid at school is that it illustrates a profoundly important truth about people. Nobody wants to be an outsider. Everyone wants to feel valued and accepted. We all want to be a part of something whether that is a family, friends, colleagues, or a church congregation. This is because we are meant to be connected. When we feel like outsiders, we can't see that what make us different makes us special. Instead, we try to fit in any way possible, defaulting to a survival mode at each new school.

Another take-away from my moving experience is that I learned that contentment and joy were always available, no matter whether I was in a new school or unpacking my belongings in my bedroom. Joy and contentment were always just a feeling away. My discontent with my high school experience was not unlike many of the adults that I have counselled and coached: "Why can't I find a fulfilling career? Why do I feel stuck? Why can't I have a successful business and a happy family life?"

The answer is, they can, and you can. Your success is an inside job. It is derived from the same place as joy and contentment. The journey to understand you begins with reflection. The goal is enlightenment, inspiration, and transformation. Finding your *it* begins with a deep dive past other's expectations, social norms, or any other influence.

Let's start with fitting in with you. I asked if you could do any job in the world, what would you do? I'm sure you put some thought into that or at least had an instant thought come to mind. Let's expand on that.

What are you good at? This is our starting point. When I asked you to imagine that you had a fairy Godmother that could put you anywhere in the world, doing any job with reasonable compensation what comes to mind? Was it connected to something that you are good at? I'd like to make sure that you aren't thinking in mere physical terms like being good with working with your hands or have a knack at building things. If you are good at putting people at ease, you are the life of the party, love a challenge, are courageous or incredibly resilient then we are in the ballpark. Does the sense of what you are good at connect to your dream?

Everybody is good at something. Even if simply making a bed. To some the question is easy to answer. For others this requires some thought. I typically end my coaching session with this as homework. Their homework is to write a list of what they are good at.

The second part of that homework is to tell me why. If you are good at something, why do you believe that to be true? Keep in mind it is imperative that you set aside judgement and comparison to others so that you can look at yourself independent of external influence. For example, if what you are good at is making a bed, why is this true for you? Do you like the painstaking detail that you put into the crisp, sharp corner folds of the sheet? How about, like me you have supernatural faith in the unseen? My *good at* and why answer (my me statement) looks something like this, "I excel at having supernatural faith in what may have never been seen before because I know there is more than what has been experienced and I want to help it come to fruition."

Now, if I looked with judgement at my statement, it would be easy to rip it apart and lose confidence that this truly is something that I am good at. What's the proof that I'm good at that? What if others are better than me at what I believe I excel at? This is precisely why judgement has no place in identifying what your talent, skill, or unique qualities are. It's time to reimagine yourself beyond what other people say, think, or believe. And don't limit yourself! Please make a list of what you are good at or excel at. Sometimes this is difficult to see in ourselves. Others may have complemented you in your past on something you did or said that helped them. What was that?

Thinking upon times when others have let you know how you have helped them, how they were inspired or appreciated your actions is different than considering how others might think of your *me statement*. The reason is that we cannot help but be connected to others. Connectedness is in our DNA. Just as we are connected by the air that we breathe and the energy of the world in which we live, the quanta (invisible connecting energy) resonate in our energy connectedness. Like a sound wave that you cannot avoid, you cannot avoid being connected. This is precisely why when we feel like an outsider or different it is the un-connectedness which makes us feel uncomfortable.

My first day of school, standing in the office and waiting for someone to walk me to the classroom, met with stares as the door opened and I was introduced, I felt discomfort. I felt disconnected from those around me, like an outsider. If I allowed my thoughts to gravitate to fear, I'd have focused on not being liked, valued, or accepted. Instead, my unyielding faith helped me traverse change, rapidly adapt to my new environment and build connections. I smiled. I knew the power of a smile.

Remember my first sales experience? I learned from my overwhelming business success that day what U.S. companies pay more than $15 billion per year to train their sales employees. I learned that flashing a genuine big smile was a key to connecting and achieving. I learned with every new school that smiling through discomfort helped send the vibrational energy that I desired. Our *it* aligns our connection to others with directional purpose.

I have found that I must experience pain to drive my passion. I know this sounds strange, but passion is an emotion. Let's explore if finding an emotion is what we are after. According to Merriam-Webster, passion is *an intense, driving or overmastering feeling or conviction.* Pain as a verb is defined as hurt. Hurt is truly the connector to our purpose. The key to finding your purpose and figuring it all out resides in your *it* (differentiator) and a big piece of that is passion.

When we hurt our greatest desire is not to feel pain. Think about this in the most literal sense as in stubbing your toe. You stub your toe or kick it into the leg of the coach (I know this one far too well). Pain shoots through your body. What do you do? You might hop around? Perhaps you let out an expletive or two or a simple, "OUCH". Maybe you sit down and grab your foot, rubbing at your toe to take away the pain.

Now think about a painful experience such as heartbreak or something horrific in your life that just didn't make sense, wasn't fair, or the outcome wasn't necessary. I remember when my son was transitioning from the military to civilian. His medical insurance was in the process of transitioning and not many medical providers that were off the base accepted his insurance.

My son was helping me move and sliced his finger with a box cutter. The cut was deep, and it was evident that he needed stitches. Holding his finger tight to stop the bleeding and wrapped in a towel, we hopped in the car to get him medical care. Unfortunately, the emergency room at our local hospital did not have the best reputation for their level of care nor their expediency. I suggested to my son that we go to the local urgent care.

Bypassing the hospital, we made our way to the urgent

care. After a brief intake procedure getting basic information on insurance and identification, the staff member quickly escorted my son to an examination room. Within minutes the doctor on duty came into the room and looked at my son's wound. As soon as the pressure came off the finger, blood began to rush forward. The doctor confirmed what we thought that stitches were required.

While the doctor was completing his examination, the front office staff member had come into the examination room. She waited quietly until the doctor had made his diagnosis. At that moment she chimed in.

"Excuse me. I just checked and unfortunately, we don't take your insurance," the woman asserted. "You will need to pay cash for being seen, whether we treat you or not. We don't take military insurance. We just stopped accepting it."

Needless to say, I was completely aggravated. "What do mean? Don't you think you should have said something when we checked in? You took a copy of his military i.d. and insurance card. Don't you think this would have been a good time to have told us that?"

Obviously, my son was uncomfortable and just needed to stop bleeding. We had no choice but the agree to the terms of treatment so that my son could get the stitches. This experience, however, was incredibly irritating as I instantly recalled reading news story after news story of military veterans not receiving the benefits and services they deserved following their selfless sacrifice to ensure our personal freedoms. This type of pain typifies a painful experience that can be tapped into a passion to drive change.

When people talk about finding passion, the search is for the driver, through the pain. What connects you to your core? We use the connection to core values and beliefs to fuel passion. In my example, this experience might drive someone into a career of veteran rights advocacy.

Can you think of a painful experience that left you thinking: How can this be? This can't be right. Why doesn't someone do something about this?

Just about every invention that we can think of comes out of pain. We don't really think of improvement being derived from pain, but frustration is pain. Frustration can take the form of irritation or longing for what is missing.

"What if" is a powerful catalyst for change. "What if" has the potential to connect pain to the passion of what you excel at. "What if" can change the world and can catapult you to a career or life you love. Do you think that Apple creator, Steve Jobs, viewed his work as a job? Do you think he put more thought into what other people thought than what he knew he was good at?

Steve Jobs, a college dropout, had something he was good at. Tinkering with electronics. What was his why? I think we can extrapolate why he believed he was good at tinkering with electronics. Because he thought he could create something greater than what already existed. Perhaps he was frustrated with what existed and said, "what if"?

There is no difference between Steve Jobs or any of us. Everybody has something that they excel at. Let's begin imagining how what you are good at might transform how you see yourself. To illustrate this, let me share with you the story of Vicki.

Vicki is always the first person to give a complement. She is kind, caring, accepting of all and people genuinely like Vicki. What is there not to like about Vicki? We all would love to be surrounded by people like Vicki.

Unfortunately, Vicki can be her own worst enemy.

After years of battling Lupus and the myriad of health and weight challenges that this delivered, Vicki would continue to be the first to offer praise to others. She has a wonderful gift of affirmation toward others. Vicki continually offers to hostess home parties for her friends and acquaintances from church. These party consultants rely on the party host to invite a group of their peers or family to buy whatever it is they are selling. Over the years Vicki has hosted more parties than anyone that I know.

After being unable to attend countless parties, I finally succumbed to a candle party where she was the hostess. When I walked in Vicki's humble home it glowed with flickering candles that smelled of warm vanilla and cinnamon. A stunning feast of delicious looking finger foods, including Vicki's coveted Gooey Butter Cake, were set out on the dining room table. Of course, when a new guest arrived Vicki greeted each as if they were a V.I.P.

The consultant had many items displayed but it wasn't her sales pitch that caught my attention. If you have never attended a candle party let me paint the picture. Party guests sit around the consultant's display as items from the candle catalog are brought to life. The consultant shows how items might be changed up for various holidays, events, or décor styles. What made the items truly come to life was Vicki.

As the consultant would bring out the latest candle holder and begin to provide technical information and pricing, Vicki would chime in and tell how she used this item and how she changed up how the item would typically be displayed. Item after item, the consultant's pitch was dimmed like a solar eclipse by Vicki's glowing description. Vicki's passion as she talked about the products was infectious and sales that night were through the roof.

The highlight of every home party is an offer to become a consultant or to host a party of your own. The consultant goes into the benefits of each from free product to trips and extra income. This night was no different. Vicki quickly began to offer encouragement to the other ladies in the room explaining why each would be great at selling.

When I asked Vicki why she wasn't the one selling the candles she provided me with a laundry list of why she was unqualified. This was my opportunity to reciprocate Vicki-like praise and accolades of what I saw as her strengths and attributes. I went on to explain what an amazing hostess she was and how she made people feel special. I told her that her wonderful descriptions of items that night helped the audience visualize the candles and holders in their homes. I watched as the light came on as her face lit up with delight. She couldn't help but agree that she was a natural at selling. Vicki signed on to become a consultant and experienced wonderful success because she connected her "why". Motivating people and providing them with a vision.

I believe that this initial belief in herself is what started Vicki toward her true path. Vicki is now an advocate for parents of autistic children. She leads support groups helping motivate and encourage these family members so that they can find resources and believe in something greater for their loved ones. Vicki is in the process of writing a book on her experience with raising an autistic child, her challenges and joys. All sparked by a candle.

CHAPTER 3

THE HEART OF THE MATTER

"I haven't failed, I've just found 10,000 ways that won't work" ~ Thomas Edison.

Author Steven King, after 30 unsuccessful attempts at becoming a published author, succeeded. Technology mogul, Bill Gates first business venture in traffic data processing resulted in an idea that didn't work out in a way that he would have hoped. What that failure did was provide him with a valuable learning opportunity and an avenue to use what he learned to change things up.

Filmmaker, Steven Spielberg was not accepted into USC which was his first choice in schools. Did this stop him in his tracks or was this just a pivot point? Did this stop him from becoming hugely successful? Of course not. Why? Because Mr. Spielberg's success was not linked to his circumstance, his pedigree, or school. His success was linked solely to something at his core. How many times in your life have things not worked out the way you wanted?

Life can be full of disappointments as our expectations do not meet what happens. No matter how hard we wish or hope, somehow, what we wanted so bad just does not come through. We might think that we have the perfect plan, yet it fails. It's important to understand that these so-called failures and disappointments can serve to your advantage, but it requires a shift of perspective. Steven King, Bill Gates, or Steven Spielberg could have given up and said that they tried but it didn't work. "It must not be in the cards." How many times have you thought that?

"Oh well, it must not be meant to be."

Accepting failure as a termination point, cuts you off from the potential of achieving success. Every success is the result of trial and error, even if the error is someone else's. In the development of new drugs and disease research, errors occur, but research continues because errors are lessons. One researcher may launch a study from an area overlooked by another researcher. Trial and error provide insight and opportunity. Acceptance of failure as another chance to succeed is key.

The 2006 comedic movie, *Accepted*, provides a humorous twist on turning lemons into lemonade. The movie is about a group of recent high school graduates who are not only rejected by their first-choice college, like Steven Spielberg, but also every school choice. The disappointment is exacerbated by high parental expectations of college attendance. In an attempt to avoid telling his parent's the truth, Bartleby Gaines devises a plan to lead his parents to believe that he has been accepted to a school by creating a fake school. As the lie grows and becomes a tangled web, his friends and others who were not accepted into a school join into the fallacy and the antics begin. The teens in the movie go so far as to rent a boarded up mental hospital and turn it into a fake university so that when parents drop off their kids at school. they believe the school is real.

We often try so hard to meet the expectations of others that we lose touch with our authentic, true self. Parental pressures to achieve, usually well-intentioned, cause us to question what we desire rather than what would meet expectations. We might feel societal pressures as we accept others' beliefs in what is acceptable. For example, you might be completely comfortable being single, yet others elude that there is something wrong with you. If you are not in a relationship, clearly you must be having trouble finding someone. What if you simply don't want a relationship? The longer we are on this planet, the more time we have had to have the influence of others' beliefs and expectations leave residue in our subconscious. These external influences create a gap inside of us that disengages us with our core.

What is at your core? To help visualize your core and its relevance to your understanding you, picture an apple sliced in half. You would see a space in the middle that looks like a heart filled with seeds. This is the lifeblood of the apple, wherein the life of the apple takes shape, and the fruit comes forth. Within the core of the apple is a heart-shaped shell that protects the seeds. After the fruit is gone, the seeds are its future. Just like the apple protects its core seeds, so should we.

We are driven by our core, and like the apple, I like to refer to it as our heart-core. Within our heart-core are values that are an essence of our true being and true self. Everything that drives our being comes from our heart-core. From the seeds of our heart-core we can learn to describe, define and test our authentic and true self.

I don't believe that anyone reading this book would need to have core values defined, however, core values are worthy of explaining because they are often confused with ideals when we are trying to define them. There are core values for business, for organizations, for groups, and for individuals. Our heart-core seeds are our personal core values.

Core values might be things like passion, kindness, commitment, honesty, dependability, loyalty, efficiency, reliability, positivity, optimism, or compassion, and the list goes on. Defining your core values is essential in understanding what makes you tick. As you figure this out, we can put all the pieces of your puzzle together. What makes you, you? You are then able to function at your highest level because your *it* will be shining brightly. Below is a list of personal core values. Of course, there are more, but this should get you started. Read through the list and note all words that resonate with you. Don't overthink this exercise, simply select the words that seem to stick out to you above all others.

Initially, you may choose 10 or 20 words. Write them down. We will use these as our launching point for the next part of this exercise. Again, do not overthink. Select the words that stick out to you. Go with your gut.

List of Personal Core Values

Acceptance
Accountability
Achievement
Adventure
Ambition
Assertiveness
Artistic
Balance
Beauty
Believing
Belonging
Boldness

Calmness	Carefulness
Cheerfulness	Commitment
Community	Compassion
Competence	Competitiveness
Consistency	Contentment
Contribution	Control
Cooperation	Courage
Courtesy	Creativity
Curious	Decisiveness
Democracy	Dependability
Determination	Difference-making
Diligence	Diplomacy
Discipline	Diversity
Effectiveness	Efficiency
Ethics	Elegance
Empathy	Enjoyment
Excitement	Equality
Excellence	Expertise
Exploration	Expressiveness
Fairness	Faith
Fame	Family
Fitness	Focus
Friendship	Financial
Freedom	Fun
Generosity	Goodness
Grace	Happiness
Hard work	Health
Helping	Honesty
Honor	Humility
Improvement	Independence
Influencing	Ingenuity
Inquisitiveness	Insightfulness
Intelligence	Integrity
Intuition	Joy

Justice	Knowledge
Leadership	Legacy
Love	Loyalty
Mastery	Meaningful
Minimalism	Money
Nature	Openness
Orderly	Originality
Participation	Perfection
Persistence	Personal development/growth
Personal time	Physical challenge
Pleasure	Positivity
Power	Practicality
Preparedness	Privacy
Problem-solving	Professionalism
Prudence	Public service
Purity	Quality
Recognition	Relationship
Relaxation	Reliability
Resourcefulness	Respect
Responsible	Results-oriented
Risk-taking	Security
Serenity	Self-awareness
Self-care	Self-control
Selflessness	Self-reliance
Sensitivity	Serenity
Service	Simplicity
Spirituality	Spontaneity
Stability	Status
Strength	Structure
Success	Teamwork
Support	
Thoroughness	Thoughtfulness
Timeliness	Tolerance

Uniqueness	Unity
Usefulness	Vitality
Wealthiness	Wealth

As discussed previously, what's in us can get camouflaged as layers of expectations and societal norms influence how we think, feel, and act. Unfortunately, this effects our results. Therefore, we might feel like we are spinning our wheels and not getting anywhere. It may seem like others are achieving but we seem to be stuck. This also is why we might give in or give up and fall back into an excuse that we tried, and it didn't work. Let's cut into that apple and better understand the seeds of your heart-core.

Your heart races when you see...what? When you think of...what? What excites you? What makes you smile when you think about it? A common phrase of mine is, "That makes my heart smile." What makes your heart smile?

Now, think of when you do something that makes you feel great. Typically, this will correspond with you doing something for someone else. If you are a parent, you might think about the joy you feel when your child accomplishes something. You might think of a time when you helped someone through a difficult situation. Perhaps it was the moment you graduated college or said, "I do."

I like to start a core value discovery session by looking at what makes you smile, the things that make your heart smile. When you think about things that excite you or make you feel great, you are mentally in a perfect place to look inside of you. I like to think of it as greeting your inner-self, your true, core-self with a smile.

Look at the list that you made from the core-value list or other core values that came to mind as you were writing down what stuck out to you. Your job now is to take the initial list that you developed and refine that list to 3-5 of the words that you would use to describe you. Ponder your list for what is most important to you. Again, go with your gut and do not judge. It is imperative that you think about what makes you tick.

Your core values should not be confused with ideals and that is why it is important that you don't judge your choices. It's easy to look at the list and choose words that others would find admirable or that you simply desire were words associated with you. For example, if you cannot be early to an appointment or event to save your life, you probably would love to identify with reliable or dependable but in reality, that is not you. If you strive to always be on time, what word best describes your why? Why is this important to you? Choose the word that best describes your why.

People are complex and multilayered. Just as the heart-core of the apple contains many seeds, so do we. Find your seeds in the personal core values list. Which best describe you? If you chose the word courage, ask yourself why is this important to me? Also ask, is this something that I frequently and consistently do? How do I frequently and consistently reflect courage through what I do? What we do, even when we are on autopilot, especially when we are on autopilot, comes from the core.

Keep in mind, if you begin having negative thoughts during this process, you will need to crush them as soon as they emerge by shifting back to what makes your heart smile. An example of this is when you ponder core values like dedication or perseverance and immediately your thoughts go into judgement. You might think, "How can you consider yourself dedicated when every time you make a New Year's resolution you never do it?" Think instead of something that makes you happy related to how you see yourself as dedicated. Forcefully shifting your thoughts toward positive, loving thoughts is like sticking up for your best friend when they are being bullied. You do not have to be your worst enemy and in this exercise being your best friend is your highest priority. You are worth it!

Let's take a look at the list that you came up with. You should have 3-5 words that are the essence of your true being. These words describe you. The next step is how you define the words in relation to you and what you do. If one of your words is cheerfulness and this describes you to the core, you are most likely that person who is smiling through challenges. You are probably an eternal optimist and help point out to others the silver lining within their clouds. These are definitions of your core. Write next to your words to define your description.

Examples:

Cheerfulness – I love being a beacon of light when I enter a room. I love cheering people up; it makes me feel good. I love how people tell me that I am the happiest person they know.

Improvement – I get excited when I find ways to improve processes at work. I can easily identify where things don't work and continually seek out ways to improve upon the current state.

Originality – It's important to me that I do things differently. I love the creativity involved in originality. I'm happy when I can contribute a new and original idea.

The final piece of the exercise is a test. You will literally apply a test to each of your descriptors, your heart-core seeds to make sure you indeed have core values and not ideals. An ideal always sounds good but it doesn't feel right in your gut, and it definitely will conflict with the test.

Here is your test. Take each of your descriptors and ask

yourself this question:

Would I hold true to my core value no matter what? If someone were to offer me a million dollars to not "do" my core value, would I take the money? If someone were to say that they would have nothing to do with me ever again if I "do" my core value, would I choose my core value or them? If I were to be threatened to not "do" my core value, would I cave?

Let's test this.

You value intelligence. You are a lifelong learner and appreciate well researched information. You have invested in many books on many topics that have provided you opportunities to challenge and expand your thinking. You begin dating someone that seems to incorporate everything you are looking for in a mate. During your courtship, it becomes evident that this person's opinions are based on unsubstantiated data. This really bugs you, but you think that this is not a deal breaker. As time goes on, you learn that your mate is not interested in intellectual conversations, reading, or thinking for his or herself. It seems that what didn't seem to be a big deal previously has now become a huge deal. You feel as if your soul is crying for an intellectual conversation. You are ready to break up. Before you do, he or she reveals to you that they hadn't shared up to this point that they were heir to a multi-million-dollar fortune and a *trust baby*. Would you stick with it? Would you abandon what is so important to you for a chance to be mega rich?

You value integrity. You are a bookkeeper for a large manufacturing company. Your boss comes to you and says, "Hey, I'm not sure how to tell you this, but the company may be in big trouble. We could all lose our jobs. I got thinking about this and if we were able to show a profit on our financials to the Board this month, I think we could buy some time to get things right. You could help me change things around just a bit so that it looks like we are profitable, right? It's only a white lie. I know we are going to do better next month. I can count on you right? I mean, we don't want to lose our jobs. Right?"

Would you do what your boss has asked of you? Or would you do what you believe in your core? If you chose integrity as an ideal because it sounds good and you believe it is something that everyone should say is their core value, you end up bending and doing what your boss asked. Afterall, he said it will all be alright next month! Nobody will ever know!

If your true core value was integrity, there is no amount of money that would change your mind. I can provide you with a real-life example of this as integrity happens to be one of my heart-core seeds. I was faced with a test of this core value when I first began consulting to major banks across the U.S.

My reputation as an auditor with integrity spread from where I was working within the Western states of the U.S. to the East Coast. I was operating my business at the same time as business giants, Enron and WorldCom were making headlines. This was also a period when lending practices were lax and less than ethical. Portfolios were plagued with bad paper and maleficent behavior including embezzlement, insurance fraud, and theft were prolific.

I received a call from a woman who introduced herself as an executive with a Wall Street financial company. She stated that I came highly recommended from her Vice President on the West Coast who had met me while working on one of my audits in Los Angeles. She explained that she had a predicament with one of her portfolio accounts and needed someone she could trust. Instantly, my ears perked up. I had come highly recommended by a major Wall Street VP! Of course, my ego was paying attention. I was all ears.

The woman went on to explain how she wanted to offer me a contract to work on a troubled account that she suspected nefarious activities. She went on to explain how she would need me in Philadelphia within the next few days. "Name your price." My head was reeling. This was the big break that I had been waiting for with my business. This was the 7-figure jump for my company that I dreamed of. This could take me to the next level.

My head was in the clouds. I was instantly transported back to earth. Without hesitation, I replied, "I'm sorry, I'm not available for out of state work. If there is something that you would like me to review or complete from California, I'd be more than happy to help you out."

The woman seemed shocked. "No. I need you in Philadelphia. I need you on site. My contact said that if I could trust anyone, it was you! Name your price. Anything. Really."

"I'm sorry. I don't have a price. I don't work outside of California."

Irritated, the woman blurted, "Everyone has a price."

"I don't. I'm sorry. I don't have a price."

Even more shocked, the executive reluctantly replied, "Alright. I know that you would be exactly what we need. We can't trust anyone these days. If you change your mind or circumstances change and you are willing to work out of state, please do not hesitate to call me. I need someone like you."

As I hung up the phone, a flood of bi-polar thoughts crossed my mind. I thought how great that it was to have been so highly recommended. How much money did I just turn down? How could I turn it down? Because it was the right thing to do. I stood my ground and it felt amazing!

What I didn't tell you is that at time, I was a single mother of 4 kids ranging in age from 5-15. My family (another core value) was a top priority. I had designed my business so that I could drop my kids off and pick them up from school, go to sports practices and games, and be involved in their lives. Increasing my company revenue substantially could have been a game changer for me financially, but I wasn't willing to pay the price. I held to the integrity of holding true to my commitment and my choice to be what walked and talked like a stay-at-home mom while I was running a successful company.

By holding fast to my core values, I stayed true to myself. What I did not expect is that just a year later, I found a way to do it all. I was able to expand my services across the U.S. by contracting auditors that I hand-picked based on shared values and still be a full-time mom to my kids.

What are your unwavering core values? What is so seriously important to you? Define your seeds. Describe them. Test them. Next, we will nurture your seeds to help your roots grow deep to ground you so that you can put forth amazing fruit.

CHAPTER 4

A PASSIONATE HEART

"Be not afraid of greatness. Some are born great, some achieve greatness, and some have greatness thrust upon them" ~ William Shakespeare.

In the sweltering California summer, a raging wildfire scorches hundreds of thousands of acres of forest land. In the spring, a sapling pine emerges from the ash. Shrouded by an ominous cloud a Hawaiian volcano spews molten lava, creating rivers of black smooth rock as it cools. Over time ferns and plant-life return to the ash-rich soil. What was viewed as destruction cannot stop the seeds of life. There is great beauty in resilience, and nature is full of it.

Following a terrible accident at work which broke his spine, Isadore Ramirez was told by his doctors that he would never walk again. A hero warrior and Marine veteran, Isadore was determined that he would prove his doctors wrong. Today, Isadore, a successful real estate agent in Southern California, can often be found walking door to door distributing business flyers. Isadore's strength and determination to shock medical professionals to not only walk but lead a fully functional life mirrors the resilience of the mighty redwood.

Many would have taken the diagnosis of a broken spine and found an excuse to give up. "You will never walk again". How many times do we allow our circumstances to dictate our future and create a self-fulfilling prophecy?

Like the seeds beneath scorched earth or a fire within the soul, our heart-core seeds are destined to bring forth life. Our life purpose is sourced in our heart-core. Regardless your circumstances, you have the capacity to create the perfect environment for your seeds to sprout, grow deep roots and put forth amazing fruit.

Kyle, a young African American male, went to work at 12 mowing lawns, pulling weeds and doing odd chores to help his single mom pay the rent. Despite his mom working two jobs, things were tight. They relied on the local food pantry to help keep food on the table. Secondhand clothes provided by his church were Kyle's only source of any sort of designer anything. Kyle could only imagine a life like many of his classmates wherein the greatest challenge was which video game to buy or how to convince their parents to buy the latest celebrity-endorsed basketball shoes. At 18, Kyle's mom announced that she had met someone and that she was moving in with him. Kyle was not a part of that picture. Suddenly, Kyle found himself homeless.

Working at night and going to school during the day, Kyle was determined to break a lifetime cycle of poverty. He knew that he had something in him to make that happen. Even after earning enough money to get an apartment, Kyle decided that the tent he had been living in at the edge of town was a way for him to save money each month so that he could start his own business. For 21 months Kyle endured the cold of the winter and the heat of the summer from his secondhand tent. The library at the community college provided him not only a place to complete his homework, but also a plethora of books on building a business model, developing a business plan and how to leverage resources. As a bonus the library also provided shelter from the elements.

After nearly two years Kyle had an associate degree and enough cash to start a business. He had a solid game plan, invested in a suit, business cards and set out to work his plan. Within 30 days Kyle founded a non-profit with a mission to educate under-privileged families on the benefits of nutrition. Kyle's community inner-city community gardens gave way to his nickname "The Kale Man".

The young entrepreneur, tapping into his core values, Kyle found his passion within to drive success. His purpose became evident as he developed his plan. The hardship that Kyle endured his entire life, never knowing if there would be enough food or if he could earn enough to keep a roof over his head, might have been enough for Kyle to accept an impoverished reality and way of life. Instead, Kyle used his pain to discover what was at his core – a desire to make a difference in the world, through commitment and compassion for others. His heart-core seeds took root.

Seeds grow when they are nurtured and provided what they need. They require fertile soil, water and light. If left without any of these resources, once sprouted the seedlings will wither and die. In both Isadore and Kyle's lives, SHIFT (Self-belief, Hope, Illumination, Fulfillment, and Tenacity) happened as they tapped into their core and began nourishing the seeds. Both could have succumbed to external influences and thrown in the towel, but both inherently knew that success is an inside job. Once we create a growth environment for the seeds of our intended greatness, success is imminent.

Each of the elements of SHIFT evolve as your core is nourished by creating a growth environment for your seeds. In Chapter 3 you identified 3-5 core values (heart-core seeds). These are the pieces of you that cannot be changed. They mean something to you so deeply that when you operate from them you come alive, even in the smallest things. If, for example, you have a core value of compassion or service to others and you open a door for a feeble elderly person, your heart smiles. When we operate from our core, we feel its resounding affect – it's unmistakable.

Let's think about your core values and the elements of SHIFT. The first element is self-belief. Once you recognize what your core values are you begin to see yourself from a different perspective. You recognize yourself as if you are looking from an outsider's view. Part of nurturing your growth environment is to scan your memory for situations when others pointed out something about you that supports one of your core values. Look into your recent and distant pass for evidence from others. This is soil to your seeds.

As a success coach, an HR professional and an educator I can reflect on many accolades from those who I have worked with. At my core I love to help people unleash their true talents and tap into success within. I do this by listening, engaging in conversation and querying. In the end, the feedback is the same. "I feel great. I can do this. Thank you so much!"

Of course, receiving feedback associated from working

from your core values feels great because you are being complemented on the *heart of you*. And when you view yourself from others' complementary perspective through their feedback, it can help you validate examples of working from your core.

After pointing out to Vicki that she was a natural salesperson, she recognized it to be true. Her self-belief took root. Something lit up inside of her as she realized the *why* behind her natural sales ability – genuineness. Vicki thrives when she operates from her *genuineness heart seed*. From her work with special needs and autistic kids to volunteering at church or selling home products, evidence of Vicki's core values can be outwardly seen. Taking note of this type of evidence is the soil for your seeds and contributes to self-belief (the roots to your seeds). As the roots push from the seed hope emerges. This is the second element of SHIFT.

When Isadore was given the ominous diagnosis that he would never walk again, imagine how easy it would have been for his hope to disappear. For a man who has an incredible work ethic, Isadore never backs down from a challenge. He is dedicated to whatever task is at hand. As a Marine drillmaster he helped shape young Marines for success. As a realtor he helps people from all walks of life find their perfect home. To be told that he had broken his spine and that life as he knew it would be forever changed, Isadore chose not to take the easy road of acceptance – that would have gone against his core. Instead, Isadore literally rose to the occasion, remaining Semper Fidelis (always faithful – the motto of the US Marine Corps) to the seeds of his heart-core: God, Integrity, Discipline, Diligence, and Perseverance.

Isadore's father was a major influence on his life. He instilled a staggering sense of work ethic, pride in one's worth and family values. His legacy lives on through Isadore's heart seeds. With his seeds securely footed in his belief in himself to work hard and walk again, his hope that he would indeed defy the odds became solidly rooted deep within him. Hope illuminated possibility – the green shoot breaking from the plant and reaching to break through the soil toward the light.

Illumination is an essential element to SHIFT as we believe in ourselves and hold hope and faith close, we create a solid foundational stem. From this foundational stem burst forth branches that bear fruit. As we believe and build upon these foundational elements, we experience the fruit of our greatness – fulfillment.

Isadore's backbone was severed yet his foundational stem remained intact. With tenacity and faith in himself and God, Isadore held the course and walked. Today he stands tall as an exemplary example of strength and grit and that SHIFT happens when we nurture our core seeds and create an environment to thrive.

Now let's focus on how you can use these examples to nurture and cultivate your own heart-core seeds. Let's look at your feedback inventory. Start by writing down each of your core seeds. Next to each provide an example of feedback that you have received. Examples might be:

You are so helpful.
I can always count on you.
The world needs more people like you.
You are so creative.
You are so kind.
Can I adopt you?
I need more friends like you.
I value your opinion.
Is there anything that you can't do?

Write as many examples as you can think of. Keep in mind, without knowing it, you have been operating from your heart-core. You don't necessarily do this consciously because it is so deeply engrained. What's important is that you think of each of your core values independently and identify feedback examples for each. Each example is rich soil added to your seeds as you begin to layer the soil of validation. This is the foundation of your garden and from where you will cultivate your inspired transformation and tap into the awesomeness of you.

As you develop your list of core values and associated feedback to support how other's see you, take a moment to absorb how it feels. Take the nutrients into your soil to solidify your self-belief – THIS IS SO ME! This exercise will drive hope in the process of figuring this all out, figuring you out. A sprout just broke through the surface. Let's water it.

Water quenches thirst and brings forth life. Quenching the thirst of your seeds that have been aching to emerge from your heart-core is an exercise of passion. As we connect passion to your values, what is important becomes alive. What makes you tick takes on meaning. And what drives you makes a difference to the world around you.

You don't need to think that a purpose-filled and fulfilling life means you need to develop a cure for cancer or solve world hunger. Instead, look to quench your thirst.

"To the world you may be one person, but to one person you may be the world," Dr. Seuss.

In the Chapter 1 fairy godmother exercise, you identified a job that you would love to do. As we revisit your answer, think about how it relates to each one of your heart-core seeds. Perhaps you would love to go to the Galapagos Islands and save baby sea turtles. Remember, money was no object for the profession that you chose. You could go anywhere in the world and do anything and be paid extravagantly.

If you identified compassion, environmentalism and commitment as your heart-core seeds can you see how saving baby sea turtles might be fulfilling? Identifying what you are passionate about and connecting with your core is where you find the soul quenching hydration for your seeds.

Looking at how passion and core values connect when we can pull back and look from the vantage of our "dream job" helps us more clearly understand this concept, but what about in *real life*? This is where creativity comes in. What could you do that is within reach? Perhaps like the Kale Man you choose to make a difference through a non-profit. Maybe it's through your current profession or current place of work. How about volunteering?

Everyone is a Michael Jordan at something in their heart. This is your chance to connect your natural talents and characteristics to what means something to you and drives you. What if you have artistic talent and you are tech savvy? Maybe those folks who are working with those sea turtles in the Galapagos could benefit from your developing a website and creating awareness of the problem. Or how about if you are like Vicki and have a heart seed of genuineness. Can you see how if Vicki cared deeply about sea turtles that she might be incredibly effective in raising money to support the environmentalists' efforts?

At the top of your list of values and examples, write the following:

"I am passionate about ________________________."
Fill in the blank.

Is what you are passionate about connected to your dream job? In most cases there will be a similarity, because if you could work and not feel like you are working this is typically something that is entrenched within your passion. For example, my dream job is to run a writer's retreat from a county estate outside a quaint village in Ireland. At my writer's retreat I would provide a picturesque, serene environment wherein to help inspire the writing process. I would coach my clients to overcome writer's block and work toward making their book-writing dreams come true.

Connecting the blank of what you are passionate about to your core and identifying what you *might do* can feel like a daunting task. Fortunately, the work that you have done up to this point can be incredibly useful to you right where you are right now.

It is not uncommon for people to reach a point in their lives where they experience a conflict between their perception of themselves and what they thought their lives would be like up to that point. This is known as *midlife crisis*. In midlife crisis, the crisis is a lack of fulfillment. By identifying what drives you and what is important to you, you seize control of your fulfillment. This is because you've done the homework to put yourself in situations of feeling fulfilled.

CHAPTER 5

THE THOUGHT DESIGN PARADIGM

"Be a yardstick of quality. Some people aren't used to an environment where excellence is expected." ~ Steve Jobs

Once a year, during my doctoral program, I attended residency in Tempe, Arizona. The university negotiated a group rate for its students at a chain hotel that catered to business travelers. The hotel didn't boast lavish amenities, but the rooms were clean, comfortable and spacious, which was perfect for completing assignments. Just off the lobby was a large buffet restaurant and an attached bar. The space became the hub of student group activities such as team homework assignments that required hours of nightly collaboration. Nothing about the place would cause a person to think that it was anything but ordinary;

that is until something extraordinary happened.

Nearly a decade earlier I had been working as a business transformation consultant in nearly every major city in the United States. As a travelling consultant, frequent flyer miles and hotel rewards become the norm. I learned where I preferred to sit on the plane and how far away from the elevator I preferred to stay in a hotel. Occasionally, someone does or says something to change your experience. Perhaps an upgrade or free drink coupons, otherwise it's more of the same with each trip.

On one trip to Memphis, while coordinating audit and business valuation services for a bank owned entity with several other consultants, something happened that changed my life. I was reading the morning paper and drinking coffee in the lobby of the hotel while waiting for the other consultants to emerge from their rooms. We had a late night at the client's site the night before and everyone was slow to roll out of bed and get moving. I was anxious to get out the door because the sooner I could wrap up my work in Memphis the sooner I could get home to my kids. The events that had unfolded the night before on the audit made it necessary for me to wait to discuss the day's strategy with the other consultants.

When Greg entered the lobby, he looked as if he had lost something. He was visibly agitated as I observed him quickly make his way into the lobby, casting searching glances from left to right. He made his way to the small cafe just across from where I was sitting. When he caught sight of the hostess, he quickly flagged her down. Curiously, I made my way toward Greg.

"Greg, are you alright? Is something wrong? You look like you lost something."

"No. I'm fine. I'm just irritated. We got so busy working late last night that I completely forgot to stop on my way back to the hotel and break a bill for housekeeping. I always make sure that I have smaller bills and I just got so busy I didn't think. I thought all of you were waiting on me to meet this morning so I'm just a bit flustered. The hostess is breaking my bill and I just need to run some money up to my room for the hospitality staff."

I felt like I a basketball was thrown directly at my stomach. What the heck did Greg mean? You're supposed to leave a tip in the room? This sudden realization was an instant wave of shame. How could I not have known this? Suddenly I felt about as uncultured as uncultured could get. Certainly, I should have known this. Does everyone know this? Have I developed a reputation as the *guest who stiffs*? Was I raised by a pack of wild boars in a remote cave? Seriously, I felt like an idiot. How many rooms had I stayed in for how many years? How many hospitality staff had I stiffed? The basketball to my stomach was like a punch of shame to the gut. I knew what it was like to rely on tips. Years earlier I had been a waitress. Oh, the shame. I knew instantly what had to be done. Time to SHIFT!

Have you ever experienced a life shift? A life shift happens when an experience instantly changes your viewpoint forever. Your new thought creates a new feeling a new behavior and new results. You become different because you think and do things differently. As I went back up to my room and left a tip for hospitality, I vowed to pay better attention when people are providing a service. For every hospitality staff member that I stiffed along the way to this life shift, I apologize for not knowing. From this learning experience came something from my core. Inspiring others' excellence. I now take leaving a tip to the next level in hopes of doing just that.

Although some individuals hold strong views against tipping, the reality is that workers in service industries rely on tips because they receive sub-minimum wage or have reduced or sporadic hours or customers. Given this reality, I am a firm believer that a job well done deserves a token of appreciation. My life shift regarding hospitality workers made me think if I had no clue, how many others have no clue? I resolved that day to go above and beyond. I wanted to become known for taking it to the next level.

When I ran back up to my room, full of shame, I was on a mission to make things right. I wrote a little note to housekeeping. It didn't feel right for me just to leave a tip on the bedside. This was truly new to me, so the awkwardness was palpable, but I knew that I needed to do something to make things right. I looked at the small desk at the front of the room and there was my answer. The hotel had set me up for success. I had the answer all along with every room that I had stayed. How could I not have known why this was placed in the room? I immediately went to the provided notepad and pen and began:

To the Wonderfully Awesome Person Who Made My Bed:

Thank you for everything that you do that goes unnoticed. I can't tell you how good it felt to walk back into my spotless room last night. I don't know you, but I THANK YOU! I appreciate your work!

I hope you have a great day!

Continue being EXCELLENT!

Jolene

I left the note with my tip on the pillow and walked out of the room with the greatest sense of doing something right. My gut no longer felt pummeled by the basketball. Instead, I felt like my heart was smiling. I'm sure, if you looked closely, a sprout pushed through to the light that day.

Notes like this became the norm. I began to take special notice on elements of the room that I especially appreciated, such as the housekeeper leaving me extra coffee or an extra bottle of lotion. Regardless how small, I made sure to leave a personalized not expressing my gratitude.

Fast forward many years to my "nothing ordinary" hotel. Of course, my habit of note-writing gratitude to accompany my tip for housekeeping continued. Each day of my stay I left a unique note of gratitude on my pillow. On the third day my note looked something like this:

To My Rockstar Housekeeper:

You make my stay here awesome!

I can't tell you how exhausted I was when I got in last night and you made sure that my room was perfect.

Thank you! Keep up the awesomeness.

I hope you have a great day!

Jolene

That evening, after an emotionally draining day of classes working through the concept and design of my doctoral research, I rushed to my room to grab what I needed for the next several hours of evening group collaboration. As I bolted through the door, my hurried motions came to a screeching halt. There before me was pure awesomeness and the epitome of fulfillment.

I wasn't in a spa, a luxury resort or on a cruise. Instead, I was at the Drury Hotel in Phoenix, Arizona. I paused in amazement and great appreciation for what was in front of me. The elephant in the room could not be ignored. Years of habitually acting from my core had manifested into something amazing.

The cutest little origami towel elephant sat regally

positioned, smack-dab in the middle of the perfectly made king-sized bed. With its snout raised to the sky, I'd have sworn that the elephant was smiling at me. An overwhelming sense of joy and happiness filled my soul. Knowing that this was a direct result of my daily gratitude toward someone I would likely never meet or know, I felt so blessed to have received royal treatment for doing *my ordinary*. My little notes had become so normal for me that this wonderful act served as an affirmation and reminded me that there is no ordinary in being extraordinary when we follow our heart core. This was a truly profound and touching moment for me, all made possible by a housekeeper that chose to respond from *her* heart-core.

I was so moved by this act that I took a picture of the elephant so that I could share not only the literal elephant in the room, but the metaphorical elephant in the room as well. I shared this with my colleagues when I arrived downstairs and in class the next day. I've shared hundreds of times since then at speaking events, during coaching sessions or even casual conversations.

I never wrote these notes for any other reason than an appreciation for service that this person had provided me. Just as I tip the baggage handler, Uber driver or server, I do it to encourage excellence. I enjoy coming back to a freshly made room where my bed is perfectly made. I love the feel of tucked in sheets. I love the smell of a clean room and a tidy bathroom counter. And the best part is, I didn't have to do it. One may argue that housekeeping is included in the price of the room, but how is this different than having a meal served? Agree or disagree, I digress. The significance of my operating from my core is that I realized that I could motivate others to excellence. I was affirmed that inspired transformation is virally contagious.

I liked it and I encourage you to let the contagion of operating from your core spread from you to everyone you encounter.

The elephant in the room is that when you are your authentic true self and when you operate from your core, you drive excellence not only in yourself, but in others. From this place we can identify and define a purpose. Let me be clear. We do not need to search for a purpose in life. Like those searching in mid-life crisis, what they are looking for is articulated and gesticulated in the heart-core. Fulfillment comes as a result of the actions that align with doing what makes your heart come alive. We will go in depth on the topic of defining your purpose in Chapter 6. For the remainder of this chapter, let's focus on the topic of fulfillment.

As defined in Merriam-Webster, fulfilled is, *"feeling happiness and satisfaction: feeling that one's abilities and talents are being fully used: providing happiness and satisfaction."*

My husband and I have an amazing relationship that has evolved over several decades. One of the things that I appreciate most about our relationship is how we mutually find fulfillment in doing things for one another. This is exemplified by my husband nearly every morning. I am married to a man who loves to cook. Every girl's dream, right? Not only does he love to cook, but he is also good at it. He continues to blow my mind every day as he takes ordinary leftovers and transforms them into an extraordinary breakfast delight. It doesn't seem to matter what we had the night before or how little of it exists. Without fail, he somehow repeatedly creates the most beautiful and tastiest dishes.

I relish every morsel of his morning culinary masterpieces and make sure to complement the chef.

Hopefully it is easy for him to understand why it is effortless to reciprocate his kindness. We continually do things for each other, maintaining a momentum of caring and thoughtfulness. Neither of us *do* things for each other with an ulterior motive. We *do* for each other because of the fulfillment we derive from *doing* for each other.

Connection of our core to doing is key to finding fulfillment in life's little moments. When I saw that adorable little elephant on the bed the feeling was affirmed. This brings me to an essential piece of our finding fulfillment, what I call the Thought Design Paradigm (ill. 5-1).

Ill. 5-1 THOUGHT DESIGN PARADIGM

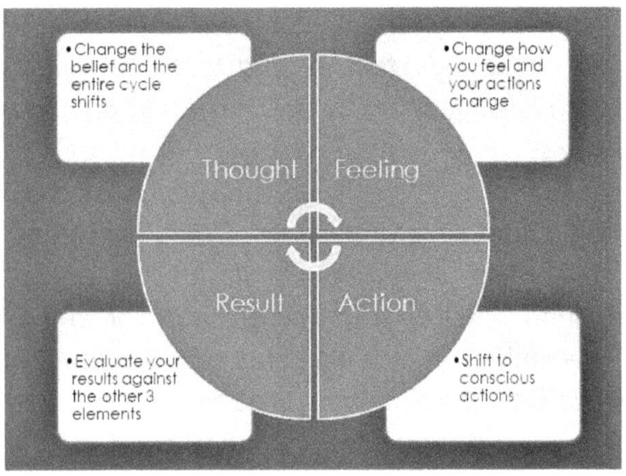

The Thought Design Paradigm illustration helps us visualize how our thoughts contribute to the fulfillment that we experience. Every thought contributes to an interpretation from within, a feeling. When we have a thought, we develop a feeling associated with that thought.

When my husband makes me one of his amazing

morning creations, I have a thought: "Wow, how does he do this"? or "Wow, this looks amazing"! The associated feeling(s) as a result of the thought is happy, appreciated, loved and the list goes on. As I explained, I regularly reciprocate, not because of his action, but because I "feel" compelled.

The compelling feeling creates a yearning within me to act. My actions then create my results. I am fulfilled and the cycle continues. We live the Thought Design Paradigm. Having thoughts, creating feelings, acting and experiencing results. If you are not satisfied and are searching for fulfillment, let's explore what you are thinking about. Chances are that your heart core and your thinking are not aligned.

When alignment of our core does not match what we *do* and when we do not think about what is important, we just move throughout our days without much, if any, thought at all. How can we expect to feel fulfilled? A purpose-driven and fulfilling life is derived by thinking about what is important to us and finding ways to act and *do* from our core. Fulfillment comes as you see the beauty and bounty from your crops. Our bounty is a result of our core seeds benefiting others. Sprout those seeds!

You were not born in this world alone nor will you leave it alone. Although it was you who emerged and made an appearance, your existence has a purpose. Your purpose is not to simply occupy space, although you are indeed doing just that. Your space and energy add to a collective of others and things that occupy the here and now, the past and the future. What you do in addition is up to you. You get to decide how to add to the collective. You get to choose the legacy you leave. Think of the funny stories and caring memories that will live on through others. When we live from our core, we impact the lives of others', and we find fulfillment through connectedness.

So how do we put all this information together? Hint: You begin to think, feel and act on purpose.

What is important to you?

Why is it important to you?

What are your natural traits and talents?

How might your natural traits and talents align to actions?

What is in your heart-core?

With these questions in mind, it is time to help you define your purpose. Rest assured, I am not suggesting that you develop a finite and pre-determined state of being. You are continually evolving as you become increasingly aware of you, your world, your *why* and your existence. Defining your purpose helps you to stay focused on the life that you desire, the life that you get to design and what that life looks and feels like. As we explored earlier, your fulfillment is a direct result of the interpreted feeling that you experience. My job is to help you better understand how to connect all the pieces so that you not only feel like you are making a difference but know you are making a difference.

Knowing is deep. When you know something, *really know*, you feel it in your gut. This creates a belief. Your goal is to believe in your who, what, when where and why. Your how becomes the fun part. How you define your purpose will help you with the magic part, living your purpose. Let's tackle that elephant in the room.

Your purpose.

CHAPTER 6

HOW DID I GET HERE?

"If you work really hard and are really kind, amazing things will happen." ~ Anonymous

What is my purpose? Why am I here? Predominant philosophers of existentialism, Sarte, Kierkegaard, Nietzsche, Camus, de Beauvoir and others helped guide a movement of deep thought and inquiry into these questions, positing their unique philosophical stances on the essence of being and not being. How can we expect to reach a conclusion as to our purpose if these legendary provocateurs of contemplation could not agree on the topic?

Don't despair, the goal of this book is not to determine why collectively we exist, but instead to serve as a strategic guide to figuring it all out so that you can live your best life. How we do this by identifying and defining your purpose for an epic effect. This is a highly personalized process and why I believe the great philosophers could not agree. Rather than considering the essence of being for all, your job is to focus on you, your mission and the impact that you wish to make on the world. Sounds far more manageable, right? How about if I told you that we will do this in just six easy steps? I knew that would get your attention. Let's get to it.

First let's start with what purpose is. The Oxford Dictionary defines purpose as "the reason for which something is done or created or for which something exists." Further, Merriam-Webster provides "some common synonyms of purpose... aim, design, end, goal, intention, intent, objective..." Given the definition and descriptors when we ponder the question, "what is my purpose," it is no wonder how you, me, and others get tripped up. Purpose is not defined in and of itself because it is not a destination as the synonym "end" might suggest. Purpose is not a destination; it is your why. Your why is not the end; it is the lifeblood of everything you do. For this reason, I like the synonyms aim, design, and intention.

Step One is to explore your experiences. The questions for yourself in this step are:

1) How did I get here?

2) How did I get to the place that I am right now?

3) Which experiences had a great impact on my life? Think of the good, the bad and the ugly. Proud moments, awkward moments, sad times and times that you felt on top of the world. Think of those moments that left a major impression on you.

4) When contemplating the rough patches in your life, how did you pick yourself up and dust yourself off and move on? What was the result?

5) When considering the greatest moments in your life, what were the results?

6) How did this change your thinking or change how you lived your life? An example might be having a child. Your life may have happily transitioned from care-free and self-focused to focusing on obligations and self-sacrifice. The moment you held that precious little creation, everything changed. Suddenly, what you thought was important was not. Another life was in your hands. You began to think differently, act differently and you became different.

When tragedy struck, what was the impact? For me, when I lost my grandmother, the loss was overwhelming. It didn't seem fair. She was the matriarch of my family. She was strong. You did not want to cross my grandmother. She was a shrewd businesswoman who wouldn't take any BS off anyone, but she was also one of the kindest, most generous and loving women I've ever known. For some reason she always had to grab your face and squeeze it like crazy as she came in for a kiss on the lips to say hello and goodbye. Somehow, she would get my grandpa to wear *his and her* matching outfits. I don't even know how she found the outfits she did. One of their matching outfits included bright neon green golf shirts with white golf pants with X's and O's. His were X's and hers were O's.

My grandmother's life impact on me was great. I learned from her to always be willing to stand up for what I believe in and don't back down. I learned that hard work and acting with integrity at all times pays off. I learned to be proud of and love my family deeply and not be ashamed to be over the top and stand out. Finally, I learned to always have a plan and to never give up. My grandmother was such a huge inspiration to me. She believed in me, and her love never wavered. When she passed, I gave her eulogy. It became clear that in my family's pain, telling funny stories, sharing loving memories and honoring her inspiring life by inspiring others was what I had to do. It was one of the most fulfilling moments of my life.

How did you get to where you are right now? What experiences helped shape you? What experiences forced change? What experiences left you different? Think back to your earliest memories, scanning for stories that paint pictures of your life. Grab hold of the brightest and most vibrant illustrations of what brought you to this point.

One of the first pictures that I grabbed happened right around the same time in my life that I had my first entrepreneurial adventure. At three years old, I found myself on stage, in a crowded auditorium in Glendale, California. With a microphone in hand and blinding lights, there was no reason to be nervous. My babysitter, Mrs. Green, the most wonderful little old lady whose garden covered in clover lived up to her name, took me to perform for an event at the Women's Club. I don't remember being coached or given any instructions, nor did I have anyone on stage with me. I remember walking past the large curtains to the middle of the stage, grabbing the microphone and I began to sing. There were no musicians accompanying me. It was just me in the middle of the stage singing Jesus Loves Me.

The crowd cheered as my acapella solo concluded. Smartly dressed women clapped and cheered from their white table clothed draped round tables. The crystal water goblets on the tables shimmered in the light. Without any instruction, I tucked my leg behind the other and curtsied to my adoring fans. I do not remember leaving the stage, nor anything more about that day, but the picture that I see was one where I was bringing a smile to the hearts of the crowd; my heart was beaming.

It's important that as your sort through the pictures in

your mind that you reflect on the feelings that each emote. Some will hurt deeply, while others will bring a smile and pleasant feelings. How you got to where you are is an assortment of experiences that have made an impression on you and shaped you. Many of these pictures serve as pinnacle, defining moments wherein you become acutely aware of your core, such as when you or someone you love are hurt or wronged. Take note of these images.

Write down a description of 3 to 5 pictures from your mind of your life experiences that stand out the most. Describe what the picture is and why it stands out. What feeling does the picture evoke? What impact did this have on you? Why? How does this picture touch you deeply?

Once you have described your memories and reflected on their impact you are ready for Step Two: Going back to your core.

In previous chapters we have explored your core values – your heart seeds. Step Two is to revisit your core values while reflecting back to your life experiences. Do the pictures that you selected connect to your core? Can you see a correlation between events that shaped your life to what you value the most? If at first you can't seem to connect the dots, go back to what you wrote down when you described your picture. With your core values in mind, reflect on how you answered each question.

Initially when I reflected back to finding myself in the middle of the stage singing to a crowded auditorium of strangers, my mind became curious. Why did Mrs. Green take me there? Had we had a conversation? Had she taught me Jesus Loves Me? I have no recollection of that at all!

Our minds are amazing machines that can problem solve and also create outcomes for event that haven't transpired. The mind creates alternative realities as pieces of a puzzle are presented. Einstein expanded on this when he said, "The imagination is everything. It is a preview of life's coming attractions." It's easy to become distracted by the playground of the mind. Knowing this, it is natural as you think back through your memories to ponder why, how, what, who, and when. Don't let this distract you from the goal here – connecting impactful experiences with your core.

Refocusing back to the stage, I remembered the crowd. I remembered the clapping and cheers. I remembered smiling faces. Why did that warm my heart so? The answer takes form of a sprout in my core; I desire to inspire people. My heart smiled as I could feel hearts smiling back. I was connected to my audience, and I knew that was exactly where I was supposed to be. I had no clue how I got there. Did we walk? Drive? Was it even in Glendale? How did I learn the song? It doesn't matter. All that matters is that I was there. I experienced it and it was an experience that is burned into my soul. Have I had happier experiences in my life? Yes! Marrying my husband, kissing him for the first time, having children, grandchildren, completing my doctorate, publishing my first book, my second and I could go on and on.

Sometimes it is the memory that you have of that experience that you still have many questions about that may be the most pivotal of your life. Why did that happen? How did that happen? I don't understand. Probe deeper into the details of each picture. Inspect them closely. Look to your heart core seeds. Why does this picture mean so much to me? What does this mean? How does it make you feel?

In Step Two we connect each core value to the pictures that stand out or the experiences that had the greatest impact on our life. Go back to the list of 3 to 5 core values that you developed in Chapter 3. Read each description that you prescribed and apply them one by one to each memory that you selected. Not every core value will apply to the pictures that you have selected from your mind. However, as you explore the nuances and the feelings behind each picture, the core value(s) that correlate will become increasingly clear.

Every memory selected will hold strong feelings. You were drawn to each one because of the feeling that you assigned to it. As explained earlier, the feeling is a result of a thought, interpretation, or story of the situation, event, or circumstance. As you analyze each picture, connect with the feeling and interpretation of what you see and feel. Which of the core values from your list lights up inside of you?

When ignited by feeling your seedlings cannot help but vibrate and send forth energy. It is as if the sun has been cast down on them after a soaking rain. You can feel them stir inside of you. Vivid memories revisited, both good and bad bring forth a stored associated emotion.

Let's quickly explore emotion as it is truly stored energy. When we revisit a memory, the energy is released; energy goes into motion – E-Motion. Energy in motion stirs you. That is why a particularly painful memory can bring you to tears decades later and an exceptionally joyful experience can bring a smile to your face, simply by re-experiencing in your mind. The stored energy is essential to bringing forth life to your heart core seeds.

C.S. Lewis said, "Hardships often prepare ordinary people for an extraordinary destiny." Within the memory of what hurts us or makes our heart ache is a link to a seed of your core. What hurt violated something inside of you? How does your description of one or more of your core values connect with that violation?

Exploring the painful events is never easy but when we do so, during exploration for connection to what is of utmost importance to us, we gain insight into the pain. We gain an understanding on why it hurt so bad because at the time our interpretation may differ from the interpretation that is developed with the inclusion of a detached perspective.

I refer to our analysis of our experiences as detached perspective because it is our intent to look at the feeling that we have prescribed, why it hurt, and then analyze the feeling to identify how it connects and violates our core values. When you go back through your memories, regardless of the span of time that has elapsed, you are transported right back to the feeling. Therefore, we make statements like, "I remember it like it was yesterday." There is no space and time.

Within the mind, space and time are all one. For this reason, some get stuck on the past memory and feeling. When we analyze our memories for their attachments to our core, we detach as if we are a spectator. Think of yourself as an art critic that is interpreting the theme that is presented in the picture. Your job is to interpret what the artist is saying. If one of your core values is truth and your painful experience is how you were wronged through a horrific fallacy, the art critic can identify the theme – a violation of truth.

The Oxford Dictionary defines violate as: "to break or fail to comply with (a rule or formal agreement); fail to respect (someone's peace, privacy, or rights); treat (something sacred) with irreverence or disrespect." With these in mind, you can see how when we look at our pain to identify how our core was violated, that we are truly illuminating something sacred inside of us that was disrespected.

You, as the artist, selected the picture of the horrific event. It hurt you deeply and you, the critic, evaluates the scene. If the playground of the mind kicks in, looking for blame and explaining why this happened, the critic can become confused by the scene that is presented. The driving theme becomes blurred from mixed messages. It is your job, as the artist, to help guide the critic by providing a thoughtful narrative by presenting why you selected this picture and how, in the present, it makes you feel. The critic is guided by the narrative. It is not just what is visually presented at face value; the narrative helps the critic better understand what was behind the art that you have selected. The more you can provide description behind the emotion, the critic in you is guided to identifying themes. Again, energy in motion. You become the driving force in guiding the interpretation of themes.

Exploring your core values in relation to your most heart-breaking and heart-warming memories is liberating as your heart core seeds burst forth with new emotion. No longer does pain need to hold you back. Instead, connecting the pain to your core values will provide energy to put into motion a new direction. This helps you get unstuck from the connection to the old feeling of *what is*, or worse yet, *what was* that becomes *what is*, to the liberation of what you were meant to do with it – learn why it holds great meaning and make it valuable.

It's not that our painful memories are more deserving to be valued than our happy memories, but like any lesson learned through trial and error, it is usually through failure that we find the most growth. We get stuck on what didn't go as planned much easier than what did, because, as I explained previously, the playground of the mind is busy in the background trying to problem solve. We ask ourselves why and how did this happen? What if? Instead of standing back and saying, what does this mean? What in my core is this moving? How has this violated me?

When we connect our core to our most vivid memories, we align the resources needed to design our best life. The liberation gained by illuminating your heart core is energizing. Your success is at your core.

Once you have identified the themes of your memories and linked them to the seeds of the heart of who you are, we can move on to the third step in figuring this all out. Step two is one of the most enlightening steps which will help you realize more about your true and authentic self than you ever realized was right under your nose.

I can't help but notice, when I go through step 2 and explore the pictures of my mind, just how the true me is so recognizable. One of my favorite photographs from my childhood is from when I was a baby, just old enough to sit up. I'm in a red, fluffy dress, with a white collar and apron. The photograph is me proudly sitting on my own. There is nobody else in the picture. I can imagine that I was placed into position by my mom and dad as they backed and made noises to get me to look at the camera and smile. Not only do I have a beaming smile, but my arms are outstretched as if I am wanting to embrace the world. Almost every baby picture of mine, I have this same pose. The non-verbal, yet very verbal communication emitted, "Ta-da! Let's do this!"

My heart core seeds are inspiration, passion, confidence, and authenticity. Not only the pictures from my mind, the good and the bad, support my heart core, but my baby pictures reinforce my mission and purpose. In Chapter 7, we will explore where we have been to get to where we want to be so that we can better understand our mission and purpose.

"Happiness is not out there; it's in you," Anonymous.

CHAPTER 7

BECOMING YOU

"The flower doesn't dream of the bee. It blossoms and the bee comes." ~ Author Unknown

Step 3 is an assessment of your current reality compared to where you wish to be. This is not simply reviewing where you are compared to where you want to be, but a critical reflection on past dreams and desires. An identification of what unique aspects of you that you have been curating, perhaps without even realizing. From the moment we are born we are learning and developing or curating our uniqueness.

The purpose of Step 3 is to allow you to blossom, thrive, and most importantly contribute to the beauty of the world in which you live. You will do this through identifying your skills, talents, and strengths – those unique skills that you bring to the table and then consider how you might use those to take you from where you are to where you would like to be.

In this step, as you identify what has got you to where you are, you will be amazed by just how much growing you have been doing your entire life. The best part is that regardless of your circumstances, your socio-economic environment or even how privileged or challenging life has been, everything has been part of your establishing strong roots. It's now time to identify the fruits that you bare and how to use these for your greatest fulfillment.

When I was nine years old, I dreamed of being a veterinarian. It wasn't just a dream; it was an all-consuming obsession to help protect the lives of the precious creatures that entrusted humans to care for their health and welfare. I spent countless weekends at the local library and evenings curled up on the couch with my nose in some sort of animal book.

With a deep love of furry creatures of all types, shapes and sizes, the thought of one day becoming a veterinarian set a passion inside of me on fire. It seemed like every hurt or lonely creature crossed my path and it was my mission to help. I regularly felt like a Dr. Doolittle of sorts. From my own pets to strays, I felt a strong connection and deep sense of compassion and obligation to care. I could regularly be found playing vet. I was transported into a place where I was helping fix hurt limbs, stitching cuts and providing comfort and care.

I'm not quite sure at what age the desire to become a veterinarian waned, but I never had a time where I wasn't passionate or interested in something. One passe desire made way to another all-consuming interest after another. I still love animals, but at some point, a career as a vet became overshadowed by something else that I connected with. Many people are like me, having had a myriad of interests and desires throughout their childhood and even into adulthood. However, some people have held fast to a single path from their earliest childhood memories. Regardless, how many interests explored, or dreams dreamt along the way, the muscles of our talents, skills and strengths are developed and gets us to where we are today.

Where you are now is a result of your experiences, accomplishments, failures, learning, unlearning, honing, focusing, seeking, dreaming and so on. Where you wish to be, simply hasn't been experienced yet and is built upon the muscles that you have developed along the path that brought you here. These muscles are what make you uniquely you.

Your strengths, talents and skills may be obvious, and others demure, elusive or even obscured from your perception. Remember Vicki? It took an outside perspective to point out a natural skill. She did not recognize what a natural salesperson she was. That is the beauty of Step 3 as the insight about what lights you up (Step 2) and puts an extra beat in your heart is enhanced by re-assessing those pictures (memories) to identify how your talents, skills and strengths were brought out or developed through these experiences.

I shared that my heart core seeds are inspiration, passion, confidence and authenticity. If we review the memories, dreams and interests that I have shared thus far, including the stories from Step 2, I believe you will be in a better position to recognize how to identify natural or developed talents, skills and strengths and how they relate to the core.

An obvious strength of mine is my confidence. I have a deep belief in manifesting the unseen (what hasn't happened yet) with what I desire (what is yet to be). Remember my first entrepreneurial stint at the age of three? I had a *magic money machine* and I believed that I could use the machine to get money – and I did! My entrepreneurial spirit is rooted in my confidence that I can accomplish whatever goal I wish to pursue, regardless of what anyone thinks. I am known for planning and going for it.

So, what on earth does dreaming to be a veterinarian at age nine have anything to do with my core? Let's look at the major themes: dedication (all-consuming thinking) and compassion. I held a belief (confidence) that I could do anything and so I decided that a veterinarian sounded like a career that I would enjoy. I dedicated every spare moment to learning about animals and spending time with animals. I was tactically applying my knowledge through a hands-on application of caring for animals. I enabled a growth environment for my confidence and passion core seeds which helped me to develop strengths, talents and skills. Again, I had a plan and set out to accomplish the goals of my plan. It's okay that I changed my mind along the way. I still developed skills along the way, which were essential to me fulfilling my purpose.

When Vicki shared decorating ideas about various candle party items with the attendees, she was not only illuminating her core of helping others (she helped people envision what they couldn't see) through her creativity, authenticity and genuineness, she was also developing her natural talent of selling. When it was pointed out to her that she was a natural, she recognized that talent within herself. She then decided to further develop and work that talent. And she was a rockstar!

When the housekeeper created the origami elephant and placed it perfectly on my bed, her creative skill was evident. When did she learn to do this? How long did it take to learn? How many elephants had she made before?

Does she know how to make other animals out of towels? These are all valid questions. They all attempt to identify how her skill was developed and the extent of her level of skill. This is precisely what we need to do for ourselves – figure out or skills and how we developed them.

First, you will start by asking yourself some very important questions to help you through this process, however your questions will be framed as statements. The key to completing these statements is to go with the first thing that pops in your mind.

1) Instead of what energizes me, you will be stating, "I get energized by……"
2) Instead of what do I love, you will be stating, "I love to……"
3) Instead of what do I like to do that makes me feel great, you will be stating, "It feels great when I….."

In making these statements we are looking for insight into your skills, strengths and talents. For example, "I get energized by helping people figure out how to achieve their dreams." Why this is important to me is because when I think about my heart core, inspiring and motivating others comes from my core. I get energized by this because I am firing up my core. When we light up what is deep inside, we get energized. This is when work doesn't feel like work, because you love what you do.

Conversely, when we diminish our inner fire by not holding true to or not using our skills and talents, we can feel lost, de-energized and uncomfortable. This is when work feels monotonous. You have been developing what you are good at all your life, so why not use it?

One of the most impactful statements on my life was made by my grandmother when I was going through a breakup just out of high school. Of course, my decision around how and when to breakup was made emotionally, and I really didn't think past the initial break up. There were many loose strings that needed to be tended to. Essentially, I made things much harder on myself than I needed to. As I was attempting to give my grandma a *poor me* story, instead of joining in on my pity party, she stated, "Well you really didn't plan that out very well." Point is, I had no plan.

My grandmother's statement hit me like a ton of bricks. Why? Because not planning goes against my true self. I'm the type of person that has a plan for a plan. Her words struck me at my core. By not planning, I had no direction. One of my strengths is in my ability to develop solid plans and active steps to achieve it. I am energized by helping people come up with a gameplan to finally get things done.

Not using my planning skill, a skill that I had been developing for years, caused me to have to go through discomfort that wasn't necessary at that level if I had a plan. Have you ever said to yourself, "I know better than that"? These statements are important to pay attention to because they typically point to a violation of your core. Your inner self is telling your outer self, "Hey, pay attention to your core!" Rather than feeling energized, these core violations cause you to feel drained. They are defeating.

It's important to remember that everyone is a Michael Jordan at something. What are you energized by? What do you love? What makes you feel great? What is the talent, skill or strength that you are energized by? Do you like solving problems? Are you a good listener? Does creating something make your heart skip a beat?

When we identify our strengths, talents and skills and find a direct correlation to what is most important to us, we have the necessary components to turn our dreams into reality. What you are good at comes from life experience. Throughout your life you have honed your skills, but you may not be applying them in a way that is fulfilling or even recognizing the skills that you have. This is where looking at your impactful stories, as well as your dreams, helps illuminate your strengths, talents and skills.

Examples of personal skills, talents, strengths include, but are not limited to:

Accountable	Accuracy
Adaptability	Articulate
Artistic aptitude	Assertive
Assertiveness	Attentiveness
Authenticity	Building Connections
Capable	Collaborative
Commitment	Compassionate
Competence	Confidence
Conflict management	Conscientiousness
Considerate	Creativity
Critical observation	Critical thinking
Curiosity	Decision making
Dedication	Desire to learn
Diplomatic	Drive
Dynamic	Effective communicator
Emotional Intelligence	Empathy
Encouraging	Ethical
Ethical	Flexibility
Flexible/Dependable	Functions well under pressure
Generosity	Good attitude
Helpfulness	Honest
Honesty	Humble
Inclusive	Independent
Influential	Innovation

Insightful	Inspirational
Integrity	Interpersonal Skills
Intuitive	Knowledge management
Leadership	Listening
Logical thinking	Loyal
Management	Meets deadlines
Memory Skills	Motivating
Negotiation	Nonverbal communication
Outgoing	Passion
Patience	Perceptive
Performance management	Personal Development
Persuasion	Positive work ethic
Practical	Problem-solving
Process improvement	Professional
Punctual	Quick-witted
Realistic	Reflective
Relationship building	Reliable
Research	Resourcefulness
Respectful	Responsible
Results-oriented	Self-awareness
Sense of humor	Silly
Sincere	Sociable
Sports	Storytelling
Stress management	Teachable
Teaching	Team player
Teamwork	Tech savvy
Thinking outside the box	Time Management
Tolerance of change and uncertainty	Tolerant
Trainable	Troubleshooting
Trustworthy	Understanding
Value education	Verbal communication

Willing to accept feedback	Willingness to learn
Works well under pressure	

Once you have identified your talents, strengths and skills through your personal ignition statements, write them down. I wondered how the housekeeper learned her skill. I suggest you ask yourself for examples of what events in life helped you develop that skill? Think of your impactful memories whether good or bad. How were any of your talents, strengths and skills developed or tested? From here we can move to Step 4.

Step 4 is the development of how you build a bridge between where you are now and where you desire to be. A bridge defines what you are lacking so that you can achieve whatever it is that you desire. A bridge statement begins with:

I am passionate about....

I am excited by.....

I love to.....

I am energized by.....

Have you ever amazed yourself by doing something that you never thought you could do? We've all heard inspirational stories of people who push themselves beyond what they thought was possible and achieved the improbable. Even if you have never attended a Tony Robbins seminar, most of us have heard tales of attendees at these types of transformation workshops walking across hot coals or glass without being hurt. How about basic training for the military or Navy Seal training? People breaking past mental barriers and amazing themselves as they achieve what they may have doubted they could do. Think about when you have amazed yourself or been amazed by someone else.

Building a bridge helps you experience moments of amazing yourself. Let me give you an example. In a scenario with someone walking across hot coals, the person must focus on what they want and not let fear keep them from achieving. They make up their mind that they are going to do something that they would ordinarily fear, pushing past fear and into amazement. The difference between ordinary results and extraordinary results is willingness to do things in an extraordinary way and do things that the ordinary person would not do.

When I was a year into my doctorate program, our professor at residency told my cohorts and I that only 2% of students that enter the program complete their dissertation and become doctors. I was shocked. I could not imagine investing that much time and money and not finish. What's important is that although I was committed and confident that I could achieve, I needed a plan so that I would not end up like the 98%. What could get me, and any of you, to the finish line is building a bridge from here to there through a bridge statement.

A bridge statement fills the gap between here and there by taking what fires us up and determining what is needed to create a fulfilling plan. Let's look at what my personal ignition statement and bridge statement looked like to get me from year one residency to doctor status.

Personal Ignition Statement: "I get energized by knowing that I will be a doctor within the next 3 years."

Having a goal to focus on and being energized is one thing, but HOW was I to become a doctor? Of course, I needed to complete the academic portion of my program, but how exactly was I going to dodge distractions or life happenings and complete my research, dissertation, and pass my oral defense to become a doctor.

This is where the bridge comes in. What separates our current state from the future are the details of knowing how to come up with a plan and those need to be identified through the bridge statement.

Bridge Statement: "I get energized by knowing that I will be a doctor within the next 3 years, but I know this will require sacrifice and commitment on my part to complete my research regardless of how many challenges I face along the way."

I can't tell you how many challenges that I encountered during my program that would have stopped most people in their tracks. Becoming a doctor was incredibly important to me as I knew that the credentials would help me in my ultimate life's purpose. The skills that I needed to dig deep were my steadfastness, commitment and dedication. My bridge statement was used to help me "get real" with what was needed.

Think of the bridge statement as your "but" statement. "I want to but....." What if your personal ignition statement goes something like this: "I am passionate by owning my own hair salon." Perhaps you have been doing hair for years and have an extensive client list. What knowledge or resources are you lacking? This will go into your bridge statement.

"I am passionate about owning my own hair salon, but I don't know where I will come up with the money to pull it off."

This gives you a great jumping off point to cross your bridge from here to there. You have the talent and the clients. When you figure out the money part you are well on your way to living your dream. Maybe your plan begins by building a business plan and setting up a meeting with the Small Business Administration to discuss funding options. Or maybe you talk with other salon owners about how they were able to open their salons. Your bridge statement is used to identify what is needed. You are also going to reflect on the talents and skills that you will pull from to cross that bridge.

Figuring out what fills in the gap between here and there is what gets you to the other side. “But I don’t know how to” or “but I don’t know where,” or “but I don’t know what,” are now powerful phrases. They are the supports of your bridge and will help you find your way across to the future you desire.

Steps 3 and 4 are used to figure out where you are, where you want to be and how your unique skills, talents and strengths can be further developed or leveraged to live your best life. Up to this point you have explored what is important to you and the impact of life’s experiences on shaping you into the person that you are. Steps 3 and 4 help you to see past your circumstances and identify steps to get you closer to fulfillment.

“You must do the thing you think you cannot do,” Eleanor Roosevelt.

CHAPTER 8

LIVING ON PURPOSE

"Life isn't about finding yourself. Life is about creating yourself." ~ Anonymous

Why am I here? What is my purpose? I know I'm supposed to do something much bigger than what I am doing, but I'm not sure what that is. I feel stuck. How do I figure out what I'm meant to be doing?

Perhaps you have had these questions and thoughts. Rest assured you are not alone. These are age old questions, and as you are contemplating the reason for your existence, you are changing your brain's chemistry. The simple fact that you are seeking answers indicates that you are engaging the tools necessary to figure it out.

The fornix is the brain's critical infrastructure that connects all areas pertinent to inquiry, learning and understanding. The hippocampus, the hub of memory, is a key area within the fornix. This is our curiosity network and is driven by the brain's reward chemical, dopamine. Curiosity is based on a state of self-motivation – *I want to know*. Your desire to know, to understand and to find answers triggers dopamine, which lights up your curiosity network.

Neuroscientists have found that creativity serves as a natural anti-depressant, reduces anxiety and has an overall calming effect and increases focus. Creativity has been positively linked to mental health and well-being. As we search to identify our purpose and search for meaning, we positively impact our mental and physical health.

I preface Step 5 with this explanation of brain chemistry because, as I'm sure you are becoming aware, soul-searching does not always feel great. In fact, diving into past challenges and bad experiences can drum up a whole host of negative feelings. However, as you reflect upon those events and circumstances in your life that have influenced the place that you are right now, the process of deriving meaning, learning and discovering will, by nature, help you find peace. In addition, Step 5 is a deeply fulfilling stage as it is what I refer to as the *light bulb stage*. This is the stage where everything that you have been digging up is pieced together to provide you with a picture of your purpose. Suddenly, the light bulb will come on and illuminate your beautiful creation.

In Step 1 you looked to your past to reveal what has had an impact on your life, both negative and positive. Step 1 is an exploration of accomplishments and failures, learning, growing and sticking points. We are all shaped by our experiences. These life lessons, whether we had not realized until now just how much of an impression they have made, became the key to unlocking answers in Step 2.

Step 2 is your search inward and connected to what is

most important and how that came to be. Step 2 is the cutting in half of the apple to reveal the beautiful heart core full of seeds of truth – the truth of you. Within your heart core lies the basis for the authentic you and the values that drive you. It is within the seeds of your core that you hold what is most precious to you. This is where your passion is rooted and the impacts from Step 1 that breathe life into your heart-core seeds.

Where you currently are is not necessarily where you desire to be, and this is the point of Step 3. This step enables you to look beyond your current circumstances and reality and envision what you would like to experience. No different than your childhood dreams of becoming an astronaut or Olympian, Step 3 begins to fire up your imagination. A key component of Step 3 was for you to review the events that had an impact on your life to identify skills, strengths and talents that were shaped as a result of these experiences. You learned that you have been building skills and talents as you have been accomplishing victories and overcoming challenges.

In Step 4 you assessed how to bridge the gap between here and now and the future that you desire. In assessing what you find passion or meaning from or what excites you, you learned that you need to identify what you don't know. By identifying what skills or knowledge that you need to reach the other side of the gap, the distance between where you are and where you'd like to be becomes shorter, as you can begin to see the pathway across the bridge.

Although Step 4 enables you to gain clarity on what needs to be done to get from here to there, in no way does that mean that the future that you desire will be a simple journey or bump-free road. Quite often what we want most and what we find the most meaning from requires some sort of sacrifice in route to achievement. Sacrifice, however, does not need to take on a negative connotation; it simply means that things that get in the way of what you really want are less important and your focus becomes intent on the path that you have illuminated over the bridge.

You may have heard the acronym for FOCUS. Follow One Course Until Successful. When you focus on the steps necessary to get across the bridge, even if your footing slips from distractions and life, you don't lose sight of the prize on the other side. You can see the way across – following one course until successful.

Your path becomes even more clear as your cadence is developed in Step 5, and you begin to dance to the beat from your heart core. Each step you take will be to your uniquely curated cadence. Websters defines cadence as "a rhythmic sequence or flow of sounds in language; the beat, time or measure of rhythmical motion or activity." It's time to develop your purpose statement, your cadence. It's time to pull together your past, your now, your future and your heart to develop the song that guides your steps across the bridge to fulfillment.

Your cadence is a result of refinement. In Chapter 3 you identified your heart core seeds. You chose core values that stood out to you and that resonated within you. These simple words were power-packed with something that connected to your core; they were far from simple as you began to define their meaning. You defined your core through excitement, love or importance statements. Articulating the meaning behind each word, "I feel excited when..." breathed life into your words and reinforced the significance of each in your heart.

Depending on how many core values you chose and how many definitions you completed, the next step may need some enhancements or refinements. Typically, 3 to 5 core values are ideal, but there truly is no right or wrong amount. In my experience working with my clients, 3 to 5 seems to be the very manageable, magical number. If you only chose 2, revisit the list and go back through the steps in Chapter 3 and then come back to this chapter. If you chose more than 5, as we go through this exercise, it may become apparent to you that winnowing down to the words that really jump out at you may be necessary. Don't worry if you get working on Step 5 and you realize that you need to revisit how many values you have. You will just know, deep in your gut, when you have it right. The light bulb will come on, and suddenly everything in your life will make sense. You will know when you know.

The 1st step in Step 5 is to ask yourself, "Why do I exist? Why am I here? What is at the essence of my being?"

Look at each of your core value definitions. How do your definitions address these questions? If one of your core seeds is dependable, you might have a definition like, "I love that other people can count on my dependability." Or perhaps you have a core of knowledge seeking. Your definition might look like, "I get excited to learn new things and share my knowledge with others." If a core word that jumped out at you was caring for others, you might have defined this value as, "Caring for others is important to me because it makes my heart smile."

How do any of these statements define your purpose? Why do you exist? Why are you here? What is at the essence of your being?

Let's rephrase your definitions. "I exist to illustrate to others that there are people who we can count on. I bring hope and I encourage." Or "I am here to learn so that I can share my knowledge with others. I understand that "Knowledge is like money; to be of value it must circulate, and in circulating can increase in quantity and, hopefully, in value," Louis L 'Amour. At the essence of my being is care for others because it makes my soul feel complete.

Because statements can be especially powerful. Why do you believe that your core value contributes to your existence? Why do you believe that your core value is connected to your reason for being? Why do you believe your core value is connected to your true essence and the essence of your being? Try your rephrased definitions with a *because statement*. "At the essence of my being is caring for others because it makes my soul feel complete as I know this is what I was put on this planet to do."

As you connect to your definitions to your existence, again reflect on those impactful events. More likely than not, your connection between your core and definitions to your existence are related to life events. If you cannot see a direct correlation, explore the images of these events a bit deeper. To help you with this, let's look back to my memory of singing on stage at age 3. As I finished the song and panned the cheering audience that filled the auditorium, the smiling faces made my heart soar. It wasn't self-serving, self-gratification, as in, they were cheering at me, "yeah me." Instead, I connected with happy people with amazing energy and I was hooked. I look back on that day and it connects deeply to my first statement, "I get excited inspiring others because it brings me joy to bring a smile to their hearts." My word is *inspired*.

When I think back to sitting in the library in Redding, California, gobbling up every animal book that I could find, my passion drove me. I was all in. There was no kind of or sort of. I was fully committed to learning everything that I could so that I could do anything that I set my mind to. I was passionate about becoming a veterinarian. "Being passionate is important to me about everything I put my heart into because I know that by going all in, anything is possible." My word is *passion*.

Walking down the sidewalk toward the freeway overcrossing in Glendale, California, my 3-year-old self knew exactly what she wanted. She exuded confidence. "If you give me a dime, you can sign my paper." Brilliant! It still amazes me, just thinking about it. As a parent, it horrifies me that I got away with it, but that really is the point; I knew what I wanted, and I went after it. At 3 years old I saw a path. I saw a bridge and I marched across. "It excites me to do something that others don't believe is possible because I like making impossible possible." My word is *confidence*.

My grandma called me out. "You didn't plan that out very well, did you?" What a gut punch. No, as a matter of fact, I did not. I went against my core self. I'm a planner. The true, authentic me has a plan for a plan. Go figure. Here I am giving you the 6 steps to identifying your purpose; that's what I do. I plan! "It is important to me to be my authentic self and to help others connect with and be true to their authentic selves because connecting to the core of you is deeply fulfilling." My word is *authenticity*.

These words are the essence of my being. They resonate through everything that I do and have become the cadence that I dance through life to. My cadence is, *I live to inspire passion, confidence and authenticity.* Therefore, I exist. This is the essence of my being. Therefore, I am here. This is my purpose in life.

"People with purpose, goals, and visions have no time for drama. They invest their energy in creativity and focus on living a positive life," Author unknown.

Taking the story of you, understanding your core seeds, defining them and connecting them to your existence enables you to articulate your reason for being. That doesn't mean that you are necessarily doing what you were intended to do; be patient, we will get there. We still have one more step to go! What is important is that you do your homework in Step 5 to clearly define the words that articulate the essence of you. I live to inspire passion, confidence and authenticity. What do you live for? Why are you here? What makes your heart sing? Look to what you love. Look in your heart core. Look to your stories. Review your definitions.

Once you identify your true words, the words that describe the authentic, true you that encompass why it is you do everything that you do and desire to do, you are ready to move on to the next chapter. Again, there is no right and wrong when it comes to whether you have 3 words or 10, but I do believe that the sweet spot is somewhere between 3 and 5.

Create a statement with your words. You may need to play around with them, arranging them in a way that makes sense. Remember, as you are making sense out of the words, deriving meaning, your brain is activating. You were meant to create, to understand you. You have a purpose. It's not lost. It never was. It's always been with you, in you and about you. It's in every experience that you have had and in all the lessons that you have learned. It is in the skills that you have gained along the way, whether you wanted to or not. The definition of your purpose, until now, was simply not articulated.

Once you have created a purpose statement from the words that make you who you are, and the light bulb comes on, then you are ready to move to the final step – putting it all together. In Step 6 we will connect your purpose statement to *"What am I supposed to do with the rest of my life?"*

If you are ready, let's get to it. I'm excited for you.

CHAPTER 9

LIFE BY DESIGN

"This is your world. Shape it or someone else will." Gary Lew

Living a fulfilled life means living a life of purpose, on purpose. Living a life on purpose, with purpose, creates momentum by design. As you pull together all the pieces of what uniquely makes you who you are and combine it with what you are passionate about, everything begins to make sense. Past hardships and challenges become building blocks of knowledge and strength. We learn to appreciate our experiences, good and bad, because we can clearly see how we took shape into the beautiful and miraculous beings that we are. What excites us takes on even more meaning as the song of our heart beats a cadence of intention, determination, dedication and reason for being. When we live our purpose, on purpose, we can change the world.

I have a personal mission statement that I display proudly on my desk for all to see. It reads:

"To encourage, inspire, and motivate people to see beyond the seen and believe that dreams can become reality – all in the context of joy, love, and excellence – this is my personal mission."

My mission has become so incredibly clear to me. I understand both why I am here and what I am supposed to do. I was created to inspire people into action and take on what others say cannot be done. I was created to help people love themselves enough to appreciate the lives they have crafted so that they can achieve their dreams. I was created to help turn impossible into possible. What a mission!

In all honesty, I can also say that I haven't always been so clear on my mission. Like you, I knew that there had to be more to life than just taking up space and sucking oxygen. I knew deep down that I had a calling – we all do. We were called to this life, on purpose. We have gone through life learning the skills that we needed to fulfill our purpose and, in turn, feel fulfilled. Let me walk you through understanding how I went from *not so sure what to do with my life* to *I got this*.

In Step 5 you developed a purpose statement from your heart core words. This is the cadence of your heart. This is what is behind your heartbeat and your existence. Still, we haven't discussed how you are supposed to know what to do with your cadence.

With my purpose statement my heart core words come to life.

I live to inspire passion, confidence and authenticity.

As an author, speaker, life coach, business strategist

and human resources professional I don't just live and work my purpose, I consistently engage my purpose. Everything that I do professionally connects to my purpose, but my purpose is not simply assigned to the work that I do. Instead, I live and do my purpose all the time with every breath I take. I might strike up a conversation with a stranger about something interesting going on or encourage someone who's having a bad day. If I live to inspire passion, confidence and authenticity, I must continually look for opportunities to do this. I'm actively seeking opportunities to live in my purpose, on purpose! Once defined, you can't help but become intentional about dancing through life to your cadence.

I can say that I have *seemingly* had my fair share of luck, happenstance and being in the right place at the right time or knowing the right person. However, once I defined my purpose, I was able to illuminate my true path and cross the bridge. And who's to say that being in the right place or being lucky wasn't part of some divine plan to the road to becoming me?

By putting all the pieces of me together, understanding what is important to me and determining my direction in life, have I fulfilled my purpose? The answer is no. Just because I figured out where I was supposed to go and what I was supposed to do does not mean that I have reached the end or that I am anywhere near completing this journey and mission. But do I feel fulfilled? Absolutely, YES!

Let's explore the transition stage of Step 6, taking you from words to actions and living your purpose.

In Step 5 you identified where you are as opposed to where you would like to be. Earlier in the book, you identified what you would do if you could do anything in the world. You explored your motivations behind the choice that you made. You also explored your strengths, talents and skills that resulted from your experiences. Finally, you identified any gaps in knowledge or skills to get you to where you want to be. With all of this in mind, it's time to come up with an action plan. Just because you know where you want to go and what it takes to get there does not mean that you know the way. That's where Step 6 comes in. Step 6 is your action plan for not only figuring it all out, but getting to "I.T.", Inspired Transformation. Step 6 is your plan to make "I.T." happen!

Planning is in my blood. My grandmother calling me out with her *Captain Obvious* statement, "Well, you certainly didn't plan that out very well," hit me like sucker punch to the gut. This served as a catalyst for me to step into my purpose. As a life coach, I help people achieve their goals and it all starts with a solid plan. I have a three-phased approach to planning that I use with my clients which works beautifully for Step 6. The three phases are design, habits and reinforcement.

Developing any plan starts with what you want to achieve and getting incredibly clear on what that looks like. Design is built on engineering. Think of your on-purpose life as a well-designed building.

Roll out a set of building plans and you may see various versions based on the schematic view. You will see the scale of the drawing and specifications on what materials are needed, the floor plan and the artist's rendering of what the building is designed to look like.

Author and motivational speaker, Zig Ziglar sums it up best; "If you aim at nothing, you will hit it every time." Similarly, if you don't know what you want the design of your life to look like, how will you know when your vision comes to fruition?

When a building is designed, it is engineered for

structural integrity because the end goal is for the building to serve a purpose. Design changes may happen, but these planning changes are documented in the re-design. The builder follows the designs and only puts in the design features that included in the plans.

In Phase 1- Design, think about your *"wouldn't it be cool if….."* question and consider your purpose statement.

Originally, my question was "Wouldn't it be cool if I could write a book"? I didn't specify why or connect what I wanted to achieve; why this would be cool? What would writing a book mean in connection with my purpose? Additionally, I thought, wouldn't it be cool if I could get paid to speak? Again, I didn't have a why. I hadn't thought through why it would be cool and how it connected to my purpose.

Now let's look at where my question changed once I had defined my purpose statement. Wouldn't it be cool if I were able to help people tap into their true potential and achieve their dreams? My purpose is to inspire passion, confidence and authenticity. Can you see how this aligns? What is your, *wouldn't it be cool if….*? It's important to get very specific on what you want because the habits that you will build and the daily actions that you do, need to move the needle. If you are too vague or general, measuring becomes difficult. If you don't connect your question to your purpose, your *why* will not be addressed. Your *why* is integral for you to build habits that will support a life purpose designed for success.

If you say, "Wouldn't it be cool if I could quit my job and start my own business?" Your vision is not refined enough. What kind of business? At what point could you quit your job? Something more specific might be, "Wouldn't it be cool if I could start my own real estate flipping company and earn enough to replace my current income and quit my job?" Does this align with your purpose? Think about how what you desire aligns with your purpose. It helps to add your *because statement* so that you can address your *why*.

"Wouldn't it be cool if I could start my own real estate flipping company and earn enough money to quit my job because having financial security so that I can travel and enjoy time with my family is what is most important to me?"

Now that you have some specificity on what you want and have ensured that you have alignment with your core, take another look at your question and make a statement from it in a slightly different way. Look at your question and complete the following two statements:

1) If I were able to ______________________ this year, I would be ecstatic!

2) If I were able to ______________________within five years, I would be ecstatic!

These become your vision statements for your 1- and 5-year goals to align your *'on purpose vision'* with what you do and the habits that you will build to support your vision.

1) If I were able to flip my first property this year, I would be ecstatic!

2) If I were able to replace my current income and begin flipping real-estate full-time within 5 years, I would be ecstatic!

Your vision statements are Phase 1. Phase 1 is about

getting incredibly clear on what you want to achieve and aligning that with your purpose statement. Your vision must be specific, refined and aligned.

Phase 2 is determining what you need to do to achieve your 1-year vision. Does this sound familiar? It should. Each step has been setting you up for success. You have already put some thought into what excites you and what you are passionate about in Step 3. You have already thought about what makes up the gap between where you are right now and where you would like to be in Step 4. The difference between what you identified in Step 4 as what you needed to get from here to there, is that in Step 6 we are looking at the items from Step 4 from the perspective of building daily, weekly and monthly habits.

You don't need to worry about how to achieve your 5-year vision at this point, because that is going to become more and more clear as you habitually live in your purpose. As you work your 1-year vision by building actionable habits that move the needle, you will get closer and closer to the 5-year vision for your life.

Oxford defines a habit as "a settled or regular tendency or practice, especially one that is hard to give up." Goal is defined as "a person's ambition or effort; an aim or desired result." Finally, vision is defined as "the ability to think about or plan the future with imagination or wisdom."

Think to your bridge items in relation to your 1 and 5-year vision statements. What items have you identified that are needed to achieve your vision? What goals need to be set? What can you do daily, weekly and monthly (habits) to move the needle on achieving your goals?

I suggest that you set no more than 3 goals to accompany each of your vision statements. You will build habits around each of these goals. Again, I suggest that you start with no more than 3 habits for each of your goals. Let's look to the real estate example.

You want to begin flipping houses so that you can replace your current income with doing what you desire. You have identified that you will need to know when properties are becoming available. You will need to have a certain amount of money or external funding available to take advantage of purchasing opportunities. You will need to understand some technical elements of real estate contracts and transactions. These items were what you identified as your bridge items. These are the focus of building habits. What can you do daily to get what you need?

Bridge Item #1: You need to know when properties are becoming available.

Daily Habit for Item #1: Devote 1 hour per day reviewing pre-foreclosure listings, tax sale listings and probate sale information.

Bridge Item #2: You will need to have cash or have access to cash to purchase properties.

Daily Habit for Item #2: Seek out investors and banking contacts, identifying what types of properties they might be interested in and understand the terms and requirements.

Bridge Item #3: Understand real-estate contracts and transactions.

Daily Habit for Item #3: Take a real-estate class.

Keep a journal of the items that you have identified as your goals (bridge items) and up to 3 daily habits for each goal that will get you over the bridge. Each day make a note in your journal what activity that you did to support your daily habit. Also jot down any notes about something that stood out to you (a new idea, something cool you heard or read or something that you would like to explore) or any challenges or breakthroughs that you had. This will come in handy the further you get toward achieving your goals.

Weekly review of your habits will help keep you on track and enable you to regularly celebrate small successes and evaluate setbacks. Select a day of the week that will serve as your reflection day. On your reflection day review your daily habit activities and any notes that you made. Make a note on how you did for the week. Did you feel you accomplished what you wanted to? If not, what additional resources will you need for next week to accomplish what you were unable to accomplish this week? I provide my coaching clients with the following weekly goal reflection worksheet information to complete each week.

My complete weekly success planning worksheet is located in the appendix.

My FOCUS for this week is:

____

My Top 3 Goals this week

If I do nothing other than these this week, I would be happy!

1._____________________________________

2._____________________________________

3._____________________________________

My Daily Habits

I will do these daily habits so that I can move the needle!

1._____________________________________

2._____________________________________

3._____________________________________

Smash those Obstacles: What's getting in the way? Pick one tough solution or decision that you have been avoiding or procrastinating, and write one new habit that you will develop to resolve it.

____

Clearing the Decks!
What will you FINISH this week?

____

What I MUST remember this week:
Any birthdays, anniversaries, events, things I must remember to bring, etc.

____

____

____

My Distraction or Interruptions to watch out for this week!

____

On a monthly basis, you will review your weekly reflections and adjust daily habits and activities based on what you determine is needed.

Phase 3 is Reinforcement. In this phase you will reinforce any habits and identify any areas for refinement or re-design. Remember, designs can be changed if you realize your vision did not include something important. If you deem it necessary, make a design change.

Progress this week?

What specifically have I already achieved, progressed – what are my successes and *wins?*

1.

____

2.

____

3.

____

What am I proud of this week?

What do I need to give myself a pat on the back for this week?

1.

____

2.

____

3.

____

What have I learned this week?

Where were you too hard on yourself, what could you have done differently, what other key insights or realizations have you had this week?

1.

2.

3.

An important question to ask yourself when you are not seeing the results that you expect is, "What is the most important thing that I could do this week or month to make significant progress?" Then ask, "What do I need to do to make this happen?" You may even ask, "Is this really the right path? Am I doing what I truly desire to be doing? Is there a better way for me to achieve my goals to get me to my vision?" These questions help you to reinforce your design by allowing you to re-engineer in additional elements to your plan. Just because your original artist's rendering looked one way does not mean that you are deterring from your purpose path. It simply means that you came upon additional information that you didn't have originally. You don't know what you don't know, so it's okay to refine your plan as you go along.

There is no right or wrong way to live out your purpose; there is only being purposeful about your purpose. Your 3-phase action plan will enable you to set very purposeful goals and build regular activities into your day so that you will finally feel like you are living the life that you have always wanted. As your goals are accomplished and what you do takes on more meaning because it is aligned with your core, you will find even greater ways to live in your purpose. On purpose.

CHAPTER 10

THE FOLLOW THROUGH

"Go confidently into the direction of your dreams. Live the life you have imagined." Henry David Thoreau

You have been presented with a 6-step plan to define your purpose and develop an action plan so that you can get the greatest fulfillment from your life. An epic effect is not by chance, it's by design. The more designing that you do on paper by journaling, reflecting, revising and adapting will impact your results. By far, the biggest part of living your purpose is your commitment to living what is in your heart core. When you design what you want to achieve based on what is important to you, to your core, success becomes the foundation of your design.

I recommend that you record each of your responses to the 6 steps at the beginning of your vision journal. Your journal will look like this:

Step 1:

1) The most significant memories in my life are… (the pictures that come to mind when you think back over your life).

2) The events and circumstances that had the most impact on my life were…… (list both positive and negative accomplishments, successes and failures).

Step 2:

1) What is most important to me and why?

2) What are my core values?

Step 3:

1) Where am I today as opposed to where I'd like to be?

2) I get excited by….

3) I am energized by….

4) I love to….

Step 4:

1) What is your passion statement?

2) What is needed to build a bridge between now and the future you desire?

Step 5:

1) What is your purpose statement or cadence?

Step 6:

1) What is your "wouldn't it be cool if...." question?

2) What would be amazing if it would happen within the next year?

3) How does #2 connect to your purpose statement (how and why)?

4) What would be amazing if it would happen within the next 5 years?

5) How does #4 connect to your purpose statement (how and why)?

6) What goals can you set to help you achieve your 1-year vision?

7) What daily habits can you establish that will help you move the needle in achieving your goals?

After you've worked through the questions of the first 5 steps focus on Step 6, Question 1. Underline your answer. This will be the vision statement that you will refer to daily. I also recommend that you write this vision statement somewhere that is in plain sight for you throughout the day. If you are an Uber driver, put it on a post-It note on your dash. If you work in an office, post it to your computer monitor. If you are a cashier, keep your note next to the cash register.

Keeping your vision close, where you can refer to it frequently, will help keep your vision in your face and on your mind. Napoleon Hill stated, "Whatever the mind can conceive and believe, it can achieve." As you continually view your vision statement, your belief grows stronger, as does your desire to achieve. This reinforces the commitment needed to build daily habits to support achieving your goals. "When it is obvious that the goals cannot be reached, don't adjust the goals, adjust the steps" Confucius.

Business success coach, Brian Tracy, recommends that goals should be flexible enough to adjust. Don't change the goal, adjust the time to accomplish the goal. Your weekly and monthly reflection activities will help support your identification of any adjustment.

Keep in mind that some of the goals that you identify as the most important things that you can do to get you to where you want to be may end up NOT being the most important things that you can be doing. Instead of abandoning the goals, make a note in your journal that this goal is of lesser priority and that you are replacing it with another higher priority goal and associated habits.

Your ongoing commitment to achieving, no matter how small the steps may seem, will ultimately help you reach your end goal. The beauty of taking daily steps that support your purpose is that you will immediately begin living in your purpose, on purpose. Your belief system, (remember the *Thought Design Paradigm*), will be changed as you begin to feel differently as a result of your new thought,

"I AM LIVING MY PURPOSE – ON PURPOSE!"

This is your new truth. You have the tools to live the life that you desire by designing your best life on a foundation grounded from a strong core. Daily habits that support your purpose will enable you to move mountains. As you live in your purpose, "I.T." happens because you have allowed inspired transformation of the world around you.

Life doesn't happen to you – I.T. happens for you.

APPENDIX

Weekly Success Planner

Wouldn't it be cool if I could....

____ ***within the year?***

*My FOCUS for this week beginning*__________________ *is:*________________________

My Top 3 Goals this week
If I do nothing other than these this week I would be happy!

1.______________________________

2.______________________________

3.______________________________

My Daily Habits
I will do these daily habits so that I can move the needle!

1.______________________________

2.______________________________

3.______________________________

Smash those Obstacles: What's getting in the way?
Pick one tough solution or decision that you have been avoiding or procrastinating, and write one new habit that you will develop to resolve it.

____

Clearing the Decks!
What will you FINISH this week?

____

What I MUST remember this week:
Any birthdays, anniversaries, events, things I must remember to bring, etc.

____

____

____

My Distraction or Interruptions to watch out for this week!

____

Looking after You! What one action will you take this week just for you?

____

Long-term Goal or Intention
It would be really amazing if this would happen within 5 years......

____

[ ] **I have reviewed and balanced my diary/organizer for the week.** I have reviewed my diary, I know what I need to say "yes" or "no" to. I have time-based and allowed plenty of time around appointments including travel time. I have time just for me, for my health, and time for people important to me. My action tools are covered and I feel in control.

Weekly Success Planner

Page 2- Your Weekly Reflection

As you review your week make sure you complete the questions below in full. You can add more items you're proud of, etc. but not less than the required amount. It's important that if you can't find answers to all of the questions that you lower your standards until you CAN!

Progress this week?

What specifically have I already achieved, progressed – what are my successes and wins?

1. ____
2. ____
3. ____

What am I proud of this week?

What do I need to give myself a pat on the back for this week?

1. ____
2. ____
3. ____

What have I learned this week?

Where were you too hard on yourself, what could you have done differently, what other key insights or realizations have you had this week?

1. ____
2. ____
3. ____

Appreciation

What am I grateful for this week?

1. ____
2. ____

The people I will make a point of thanking this week are:

What do I need to give myself a pat on the back this week for?

____

What one thing could I do differently next week? List everything you've reviews above and think of a thing you could do differently next week. This can be anything, even a thought that you have had.

____

ABOUT THE AUTHOR

Dr. Church is a California native, mother of four and grandmother. She and her husband, a trauma therapist, live in Northern California, where they enjoy riding their Harley Davidsons, spending time with family and friends, and living their best lives.

Dr. Church is a master life coach, change management expert, human resources professional and holds a Doctorate of Management in Organizational Leadership. Her work in cultural change and people optimization has helped transform and turn-around troubled businesses for corporate giants Citibank and Bank of America. Additionally, her work coaching executives of start-ups, non-profits, corporations, municipal governments, and religious and academic institutions (including USC Marshall School of Business) as well as providing life coaching to individuals has helped thousands of people become clear on how to achieve what they desire – helping turn impossible into possible.

www.ingramcontent.com/pod-product-compliance
Lightning Source LLC
LaVergne TN
LVHW020642100826
845148LV00012B/2296